THE
KEEN COUNTRYMAN'S
MISCELLANY

THE
KEEN COUNTRYMAN'S
MISCELLANY

by
PETER HOLT

Quiller

First published in the UK in 2012
by Quiller, an imprint of Quiller Publishing Ltd

British Library Cataloguing-in-Publication Data
A catalogue record for this book
is available from the British Library

ISBN 978 1 84689 120 5

Printed in Malta by Gutenberg Press Ltd
Book design by Sharyn Troughton

Quiller
An imprint of Quiller Publishing Ltd
Wykey House, Wykey, Shrewsbury, SY4 1JA
Tel: 01939 261616 Fax: 01939 261606
E-mail: info@quillerbooks.com
Website: www.countrybooksdirect.com

DEDICATION

For my mother – a bit of a townie at heart

'THE COUNTRYMAN is one who has absorbed his social heritage and cultural tradition of his own area, has not surrendered to the impersonality of metropolitan life, and is aware of agriculture as a living art or industry and not as a mysterious earthy business carried on far away from the muck-free seats of civilization.'

E. W. Martin (1912–2005), countryman, writer and social historian

ACKNOWLEDGEMENTS

The author and publishers are grateful
to the following for permission to
reproduce copyright material:

Swan Hill Press for permission to reprint two extracts from *A Country Naturalist's Year*, published 1993, by Colin McKelvie, and an extract from *Tails And The Unexpected, A Collection of Unusual Angling Stories*, by Billee Chapman Pincher, published 1995; the *London Evening Standard* for permission to reprint part of an article by Nirpal Dhaliwal; Charlie Sutherland for permission to reprint extracts from his father Douglas Sutherland's books, *The English Gentleman's Child*, published by Debrett's Peerage 1979, and *The English Gentleman's Mistress*, published by Debrett's Peerage, 1980; Archers Addicts for permission to reprint an extract from their website; Random House for permission to reprint an extract from *Barbara Cartland's Etiquette Handbook*, published 2008; HarperCollins Publishers Ltd for permission to reprint two extracts from *The Spectator Book of Solutions*, 1993, by Mary Killen; Guardian News & Media Ltd for permission to reprint part of a 1994 article by W.D. Campbell; Quiller Publishing Ltd for permission to reprint village cricket team tips from *Out For a Duck*, by Ian Valentine, published 2010; *Ecologist Magazine* for permission to reprint part of an article on farmers' markets; Copper Beech Publishing for permission to use an extract from *Etiquette For The Well-Dressed Man* by Jan Barnes.

Every effort has been made to obtain permission to reproduce extracts but in some cases this has not been possible.

'GENTLEMEN DO NOT USUALLY LIVE IN CITIES. At whatever discomfort to themselves and their families they prefer to live in the country and then only in selected parts of it ... The truth is that the Home Counties, with their commuter population, housing development schemes and lack of foxes, are no longer suited to the gentleman's way of life ... Gentlemen prefer to live in out-of–the-way places with names like Hogsnorton-in-the Wold or Blistering-under-Wychwood and grumble about *The Times* being a day late.'

Douglas Sutherland (1919–1995), journalist and social commentator on all things posh

AUTHOR'S NOTE

This book is as much for townies as it is for country dwellers. Here the urbanite will learn all about the ways of the countryside, from how to make silage and the evils of fly-tipping, to the proper way of conducting a snowball fight and the law on carrying a penknife in public. However, with the exception of fishing, do not expect to find much in the way of country sports here – that subject was well covered in my two previous books *The Keen Shot's Miscellany* and *The Keen Foxhunter's Miscellany*.

THOU MUST NOT BE IDLE

ENGLAND'S FIRST BOOK on agriculture was John Fitzherbert's 1523 *Book Of Husbandry*. Fitzherbert farmed as Lord of the Manor of Norbury in Derbyshire for half a century. His jottings about farm management were to become the standard agricultural textbook for more than two hundred years. He noted: 'Whoso hath sheep, swine and bees, shall surely thrive.'

Fitzherbert wrote about everything from the collection of dung – you should never use pig manure as it encouraged thistles – to the mowing of grass. On keeping sheep he advised: 'It is convenient for a husband to have a sheep of his own … and then may his wife have part of the wool, to make her husband and herself some clothes.'

Fitzherbert kept his strongest stuff for wives. Tudor woman evidently required heavy motivation: 'When thou art up and ready, then first sweep thy house, dress up thy dishboard, and set all things in good order within thy house; milk thy kine [cows], feed thy calves, sile [strain] up thy milk, take up thy children and array them, and provide for thy husband's breakfast, dinner, supper, and for thy children and servants.'

Having done all that the missus was expected to: 'Winnow all manner of corns, to make malt, to wash and wring, to make hay, shear corn, and in time of need to help her husband to fill the muck-wain or dung-cart, drive the plough, to load hay, corn and such other. And to go or ride to market, to sell butter, cheese, milk, eggs, chickens, capons, hens, pigs, geese, and all manner of corns. And also to buy all manner of necessary things belonging to the household, and to make a true reckoning and account to her husband, what she hath paid.'

Fitzherbert was plainly a tricky man to live with. For he concluded this lecture to women with the warning: 'Thou must not be idle.'

• Fitzherbert declared that a horse should have the same qualities that a man looked for in a woman: 'Merry of cheer, broad-buttocked, easy to leap on, good on a long journey, and strong under a man.'

PLUMAGE

THE ROYAL SOCIETY FOR THE PROTECTION OF BIRDS was founded in Manchester in 1889 to prevent the annual slaughter of thousands of egrets whose fashionable plumes decorated the hats of Victorian women. The organisation was originally known as the Plumage League, which joined forces later that year with the Croydon-based Fur and Feather League to launch what was then the SPB.

The 1869 Sea Birds Preservation Act and 1880 Wild Birds Protection Act had gone some way to protect birds such as great crested grebes and kittiwakes. But the SPB's founders realised that tougher action was needed to 'discourage the wanton destruction of birds'. In its earliest days the society consisted of women horrified by the plight of young birds left to starve after their parents had been shot for their plumes. Lady members were ordered to 'refrain from wearing the feathers of any bird not killed for purposes of food, the ostrich only excepted'.

The society's first president was the Duchess of Portland, a fervent animal rights campaigner. Britain's leading ornithologist, Professor Alfred Newton, ironically a fine grouse shot in his youth, lent his support. The membership grew rapidly and in 1904 the society received its Royal Charter.

Today's RSPB is not an organisation beloved of all countryfolk. While many farmers praise the work they do in conserving Britain's bird life, some landowners and shoot managers view them as interfering urbanites who are more focused on an anti-landowner agenda than dealing with bird protection in a rational way.

Critics cite the RSPB's 2010 hen harrier survey which claimed a 20 per cent decline in the UK's hen harriers over the previous six years. The RSPB declared: 'Every year hen harriers are targeted on grouse moors across the UK and it is clear that this onslaught is having a significant impact on our population. We believe that gamekeepers are killing them illegally – under pressure from their land-owning masters.' (Note the word 'masters', an overtly political term that implies the existence of the old feudalism in Britain's rural backwaters.)

Pro-country sports pressure group the Countryside Alliance points out that, according to the RSPB's own figures, there had been only one recorded alleged incident of hen harrier persecution in the previous six years. This was supposed to have happened at the Royal Estate of Sandringham, but turned out to be a work of fiction (probably resulting from a dodgy tip-off by a bird spotter with a chip on his shoulder). The alleged shooting was swiftly discounted by police.

Only a year before, in 2009, a RSPB survey had revealed that illegal persecution played no part in breeding failures of the hen harrier. The low figure of only six successful nesting pairs was entirely a result of natural causes. And the RSPB's own evidence shows that hen harriers cannot be forced to settle or breed at their own reserve at Geltsdale, Cumbria, where no hen harriers have bred successfully since 2006.

• Much to the relief of the pro-field sports lobby, the government body Natural England publicly declared in 2011 that grouse shooting benefited moorland conservation. Grouse inhabit many of the 4,119 Sites of Special Interest (SSIs) that cover more than a million hectares of the land surface of England. Today, 96 per cent of grouse moors are in favourable or recovering condition, compared to barely 25 per cent at the turn of the millennium.

REASONABLE EXPLANATION

ON ST FRANCIS DAY (4th October) swallows are supposed to fly to the bottom of ponds and stay there throughout winter. Before people learned about migration this seemed a reasonable explanation for the birds' sudden disappearance, particularly as they could be seen skimming the surfaces of ponds looking for insects.

AS TRUE TODAY AS IT WAS THEN

'EVERYONE is aware that farming by a proprietor or an amateur is, for the most part, attended by loss in a pecuniary point of view, and that money would be saved by letting the lands to a professional farmer, and purchasing corn, straw, and such other farm produce as might be required for the carriage and saddle-horses of the proprietor. Farming, however, is a great source of recreation and interest to a resident in the country; and without some knowledge of the practices of the art in the district where a country gentleman resides, it will be difficult for him to keep up a proper degree of social intercourse with his neighbours. Farming and the weather are topics which every countryman can discuss, from the humblest labourer to the most wealthy proprietor. If there are any exceptions, such persons must be out of the pale of general country society. Since, then, every person living in the country must, of necessity, take some interest in farming.'

John Loudon, The Villa Gardener, *1850: Loudon (1783–1843) was a Scottish garden and cemetery designer, author and garden magazine editor*

ADVICE TO FARMERS ...

Let order o'er your time preside,
And method all your business guide.
One thing at once, be still begun,
Contrived, resolved, pursued, and done;
Ne'er till tomorrow's light delay,
What might as well be done today.
Neat be your barns, your houses neat,
Your doors be clean: your courtyards sweet;
Neat be your barns; 'tis long confessed,
The neatest farmers are the best.

These cautionary verses, written for a 19th century English farming magazine, were pillaged from the original poem, 'The Farmer's Advice To The Villagers', by American academic and poet Timothy Dwight (1752–1817)

QUIRKY CRICKET

BRITAIN'S MOST ECCENTRIC VILLAGE CRICKET CLUBS:

Thornton Watlass, Yorkshire. Extremely crowded ground. Within the field of play is a public road with accompanying signs, six trees and numerous other obstacles. If you hit any of them you simply carry on. The road crosses right behind the bowler's arm. One of the boundaries is the hedge and the other is the wall of the Buck Inn, which features a bar called the Long Room, stuffed with photos of past teams. The club states: 'Please do not park in front of the pub as your car will be in the field of play.'

St Margaret's Cricket Club, Widmer End, Buckinghamshire. Two white posts mark part of the boundary alongside a row of houses. If you hit a six anywhere between these points it will only count as four. This is to discourage batsmen from hitting balls into the houses and gardens, which has happened many times and causes much neighbourly friction.

Lofthouse and Middlesmoor, Nidderdale, Yorkshire. One of the smallest grounds in the country. The longest boundary is forty-five yards … uphill. Local pub, The Crown, has a collection box on the bar for contributions to the cost of cricket balls.

Chorleywood, Middlesex. The club has a hefty insurance policy because of the frequency of balls hitting passing traffic on the busy A404 which borders the ground. A tree lies in the field of play. If the ball hits anywhere on the tree it is four runs.

The Ship Inn Cricket Club, Elie Beach, Fife, Scotland. The Ship's team play their matches on Elie Beach with the pub acting as the pavilion. When the tide is in, windsurfers have been known to pass a few feet from an outfielder.

Norton St Philip, Somerset. The village team is nicknamed the Pitchforkers thanks to their rustic antecedents. The cricket ground occupies the field where, in 1685, Judge Jeffreys passed death sentences during the Bloody Assizes. According to a creepy local legend, a wicket falls whenever the church bell strikes three.

• **The oldest *cricket ground* in England is at Newenden, Kent.** Cricket, or something like it, has been played here since the Middle Ages. A local rule states that hitting a six from the pub end must clear the River Rother and land in the next county – East Sussex – in order to qualify. **The oldest *cricket clubs* are the Mitcham and the Hambledon,** both around 400 years old.

• **The pavilion at Kirkby Malzeard cricket club in Yorkshire** was part funded by American singing legend Bing Crosby, who used to shoot grouse on the nearby moor during the 1970s. He played cricket there once, the only time he ever played the game.

• **Ten tips for making your life easier in the village cricket team:**

1. Join net sessions in March and April – it gives you time to bed in.
2. Offer to help with the pitch. Most of the other players won't.
3. Don't throw a wobbly if you have to bat number nine or bowl third change.
4. Contribute to the tea – it's the easiest way to impress team-mates.
5. Umpire, if you are able, but don't be tempted to win popularity by being biased.
6. Don't drop out the evening before a match.
7. Pay your match fees on the day.
8. Don't talk yourself up or you're sure to be a disappointment.
9. Clap and cajole lots in the field.
10. Don't take yourself too seriously.

From Out For a Duck, *by Ian Valentine, published by Quiller, 2010)*

• **Jonathan Hamilton-Jones of the Churchill Cricket Club near Chipping Norton, Oxfordshire,** on the subject of cricket teas: 'You've got to have egg sandwiches, made from free-range eggs. And home-made cake. In our team everyone contributes, so you run the risk of duplication. We once had five plates of tuna and sweetcorn sandwiches. What are the chances of that?'

• **The Victorian novelist Mary Russell Mitford (1787–1855)** loved country cricket. Here she explains why village lads always made much better players than gentlemen: 'The cricket that I mean is a real solid old fashioned match between neighbouring parishes, where each attacks the other for honour and a supper, glory and half-a-crown a man. If there be any gentlemen amongst them, it is well; if not, it is so much the better. Your gentleman cricketer is in general rather an anomalous character. Elderly gentlemen are obviously good for nothing; and young beaux are, for the most part, hampered and trammelled by dress and habit; the stiff cravat, the pinched-in waist, the dandy-walk. Oh, they will never do for cricket! Now, our country lads, accustomed to the flail or the hammer (your blacksmiths are capital hitters), have the free use of their arms; they know how to move their shoulders; and they can move their feet too. They are so much better made, so much more athletic ... Here and there, indeed, one meets an Old Etonian, who retains his boyish love for that game which formed so considerable a branch of his education; some even preserve their boyish proficiency, but in general it wears away like the Greek, quite as certainly, and almost as fast; a few years of Oxford, or Cambridge, or the continent, are sufficient to annihilate both the power and the inclination. No! A village match is the thing, where our highest officer – our conductor (to borrow a musical term) – is but a little farmer's second son; where a day labourer is our bowler, and a blacksmith our long-stop.'

ANY KIPPERS LEFT?

ON THE BASIS that the Keen Countryman's perfect breakfast is a brace of generously buttered kippers, it is worth reprinting this excellent letter to *The Times*, published 12th June, 1951:

> 'Sir, If at breakfast a kipper is spread out on your plate with its tail on the right, the backbone is found sometimes on one side, sometimes on the other. Does this mean that – for want of a better term – some kippers are left-handed?
>
> Yours, &c., John Christie.'

• Kippers are smoked herrings. The world's best kippers are said to be produced in the kipper sheds at Craster on the Northumberland coast. The fish are cured for sixteen hours over oak chippings.

• To cook your kippers, place them flat in a large frying pan and cover them with boiling water. Leave for five minutes so that they heat through. Serve with a pat of butter on the top and toast on the side. Kippers are best on the bone; don't even consider pre-packed fillets.

TRICK

AN OLD COUNTRY TRICK TO KNOW if corn is ready for harvesting: if you can tie a knot in the straw without breaking it, the corn isn't ready.

• Astrology-obsessed farmers know that you should only sow corn when the moon is in Leo.

FLOWERS YOU CAN EAT

Calendula: known as poor man's saffron. Adds aromatic flavour to food. Pick off the petals and sprinkle them on salads or add to pasta and rice dishes.

Day lily: crisp and crunchy with a pea-like flavour. Good for salads or stir-fries. Do not confuse with common lilies, which are inedible.

Borage: flowers and leaves taste like cucumber.

Fuchsia: bland to taste but good for brightening up green salads.

Courgette: fry courgette flowers in garlic-flavoured oil.

Rose: make jelly out of rose petals.

Lavender: lavender-flavoured sugar is strange but some people like it.

Bergamot: leaves make a fragrant tea.

Sunflower: buds taste like artichoke.

Pansy: adds colour to salads. Most memorable flavour is *viola odorata*, i.e. Parma violet.

Nasturtium: the best flowers to put in salads and savoury dishes. Peppery taste.

DECLINE

The number of people employed full-time in British agriculture fell over 30 per cent from 1996 (610,000 workers) to 2008 (400,000).

KNIFE NICKY NICKED

COUNTRY GENTS accustomed to keeping a penknife on them should be aware that they may be breaking the law.

In an attempt to prevent hoody South London gang members from dismembering each other, the government severely tightened the laws governing knives, with the result that police were tempted to overreact in cases where law-abiding citizens were carrying knives for innocent purposes.

Unfortunately, your typical urban plod does not appreciate that a pocket knife is essential for cutting baler twine, gutting rabbits, removing stones from horses' hooves, etc. And this lack of understanding of country matters was demonstrated neatly in 2004 when Metropolitan Police officers watching out for terrorists in central London randomly stopped and searched Suffolk-based banker Nicky Samengo-Turner in his car on the Embankment.

Former Coldstream Guards officer Samengo-Turner was carrying a Victorinox Swiss multi-tool, as well as a small collapsible baton. 'It is perfectly legal to buy both of these items', he explained later in an article in *The Spectator* magazine. 'The penknife I carry because I find it useful for many small everyday tasks. The baton I bought to keep at home for security

reasons. I live in a rural part of Suffolk that, although relatively crime-free, is policed very sparsely. I often hear people outside the house at night and I feel more comfortable with the baton inside the front door.'

The police were unimpressed and behaved as if they had never seen a penknife before. 'This device has a locking blade', said the constable in charge. He told Samengo-Turner that he was likely to be given six months for carrying an offensive weapon. Mr S-T was put in a police van and taken to Charing Cross police station. There he was detained for several hours before being told that he was being charged with possessing an offensive weapon and carrying a bladed instrument in public. He was given bail.

Needless to say, when the case eventually came to Crown Court, common sense prevailed. The jury found Mr Samengo-Turner not guilty on all charges.

• *Daily Telegraph* reader Trevor Bullock from Buckinghamshire summed up the lunacy of Samengo-Turner's arrest in a letter to the paper: 'I thought it would be a good idea to check the contents of my pockets and car. I found on my person a penknife which has two sharp blades, a very efficient small saw, some scissors and a nail file/stabbing device. I also found some coins (you should see the damage they can cause when held clenched between the knuckles) and house keys (ditto). In the car, the following: a Gerber multi-tool – too many potentially lethal devices to list; a pair of scissors; a small kitchen knife (I really do use it to cut up fruit, officer); a tyre tread depth gauge which has a really nasty thin point to it (the beauty of this is that you can retract the point into the body of the gauge, so that it can't be seen); and a very heavy metal cosh, cunningly disguised as a removable tow bar. More stabbing devices (screwdrivers), mini coshes (spanners), and jacks abound. And another larger stabbing device disguised as a golf umbrella.'

• The Criminal Justice Act, 1988, Section 139(1) says: 'It is an offence for any person, without lawful authority or good reason, to have with him in a public place, any article which has a blade or is sharply pointed except for a folding pocket-knife which has a cutting edge to its blade not exceeding three inches.' This provides a statutory defence for the carriage of knives a) for use at work b) as part of a national costume or c) for religious reasons (given some of the uses of knives in 'religious' ceremonies down the ages it would be interesting to know what the legislators had in mind here). There is also the wider defence of having 'good reason'. Put simply this means that a small penknife (without any ability to lock) and a blade under three inches long is acceptable unless a policeman decides you are carrying it for unlawful purposes (e.g. to hurt someone). Should the knife be able to lock open in any way or the blade exceed three inches (lockable or not) you will need to show justification for carrying it. If you cannot do so it is likely that you will be considered to be carrying an offensive weapon.

• Wise countrymen believe that you should carry a penknife in your dinner jacket pocket when going to a dance in a marquee so that, in the event of a fire, you can make an emergency exit by ripping a hole in the canvas. Before the days of fire-proofing, a penknife was considered essential evening kit before going to a party in a tent.

OLD NAGS

'For my part, I don't see why men who have got wives, and don't want 'em, shouldn't get rid of 'em as those gypsy fellows do their old horses', said the man in the tent. 'Why shouldn't they put 'em up and sell 'em by auction to men who are in want of such articles? Hey? Why, begad, I'd sell mine this minute if anybody would buy her!'

Appalling sexist stuff from Thomas Hardy's rural masterpiece
The Mayor Of Casterbridge, *1886*

ALWAYS A MISTRESS

DOUGLAS SUTHERLAND, late great social commentator on upper-class rusticity, told a story of an elderly landowner earl, who presented himself as a pillar of respectability. Every Sunday he attended church with his wife and children while the tenantry looked on respectfully. But everybody knew that the old boy had, for years, kept a mistress in a comfortable little house in a neighbouring village, for to have her living on his own land would, of course, have been out of the question. Quite simply, you don't shit on your own doorstep.

'This was both acknowledged and accepted', recalled Sutherland. 'Indeed, if anything, the very tidiness of the situation added to his reputation as a good father and devoted husband.'

Then one day the countess died. 'The only matter for speculation in the village was how long might be considered a decent interval before the earl moved his paramour into the big house and made an honest woman of her. When, instead, he married the widow of one of his neighbouring landowners, the whole locality was outraged. Even his mistress locked her front door against him, and there were few who could be found to disagree with her.'

Sutherland concludes, 'Of course they were all quite wrong in adopting this censorious attitude. A decade earlier, nobody in their right mind would have expected a chap to marry his mistress, just because his wife had become dead. Once a mistress, always a mistress.'

From The English Gentleman's Mistress, *by Douglas Sutherland,*
Debrett's Peerage Ltd, 1980

RUSTIC LUCK

The system of 'luck money', one of England's most obscure and secretive rural customs, continues to thrive throughout England, particularly in the Midlands and the North.

The tradition, which originated amongst Romany gypsies, has been practised for centuries by farmers at cattle markets and livestock fairs. The idea is that when you purchase a sheep or cow, you are handed back some money for good luck in the form of a small tip from the seller, a token of thanks to the person buying your stock. However, if you are slow to offer it yourself, it is perfectly acceptable for the purchaser to prod you with the words: 'What about the luck money?' Generally, the figure can amount to between 1 and 2 per cent of the purchase price. The sale of a £1,000 cow would thus entail the vendor handing back at least a tenner, perhaps a twenty if Christmas was coming.

• In the author's home county of Shropshire, farmers, notably muddy rustics from the Welsh borders, regularly ask for luck money. A few years ago the author sold a tractor to an elderly Shropshire farmer for several thousand pounds in cash. The old boy expressed great surprise that the author did not immediately offer luck money, persuading him to peel off and hand back three £20 notes from the large, greasy wedge that had just been handed over. This satisfied the farmer that the deal had been done properly and in the correct spirit.

• Luck money is very seldom demanded these days in the southern and western counties of England. Years ago in Gloucestershire the vendor used to place a few bob on the back of a cow before handing it over to the purchaser, but the tradition has long since died out.

• In 1965 the custom of 'luck money' was raised in Parliament when the then Chancellor of the Exchequer, Jim Callaghan, was asked whether he would instruct the Inland Revenue to investigate the practice with a view to taxing the recipients. Callaghan wisely declined on the basis that the giving of luck money was so secretive that it would most likely give tax inspectors a huge amount of work with very little return.

GLOBES AND PYRAMIDS

THERE WAS SO MUCH ITALIAN-INSPIRED TOPIARY in the grounds of English country houses by the beginning of the 1700s that the poet, dramatist and self-styled landscape expert Joseph Addison was driven to complain:

> 'Our British gardeners, instead of humouring nature, love to deviate from it as much as possible. Our trees rise in cones, globes and pyramids. We see the marks of scissors upon every plant and bush. I would rather look upon a tree in all its luxuriancy and diffusion of boughs and branches than when it is cut into a mathematical figure. I cannot but fancy that an orchard in flower looks infinitely more delightful, than all the little labyrinths of the finished parterre.'

Addison (1672–1719) was a significant social commentator of early eighteenth-century England. He attracted a formidable following of people who agreed that foreign-influenced landscapes posed a threat to English patriotic values.

• Addison is credited with the excellent remark: 'What sunshine is to flowers, smiles are to humanity. These are but trifles, to be sure; but, scattered along life's pathway, the good they do is inconceivable.'

BRITISH HAREWAYS

'I have a vivid childhood memory of Nutt's Corner, the County Antrim airport that formerly served Northern Ireland, where hundreds of hares lived out on the grassy swards that were intersected by the runways, and where scores of hares raced alongside the old Dakota aircraft as we taxied prior to take-off. The hares would also run along beside aircraft that were taxiing to the terminal after landing, seemingly enjoying all the bustle of airport life, despite the noise of propellers, and, later, jets.

'And when, in the late 1960s, all commercial air traffic was eventually switched to the new and larger Aldergrove airport a few miles away, the hares migrated en masse to establish themselves there; a direct cross-country migration of an estimated six or seven hundred hares, that immediately settled in and felt quite at home again, surrounded once more by the familiar noises of aircraft comings and goings. What matter if the engines of Rolls-Royce and Pratt & Whitney made the air tremble with the most unpastoral noises, when the place was such a perfect hare habitat in so many other ways, with wide acres of lush grass, free of all sprays and agrochemicals, and a fenced perimeter to exclude foxes and other predators?

'And just as Pavlov's dogs had learned to salivate when the feeding bell was rung, so the Nutt's Corner hares had learned that the airport din was the noise that meant safety, and then reared innumerable successive generations of hares whose first sensations must have been of aircraft activity.'

Colin McKelvie, A Country Naturalist's Year, *published by Swan Hill Press, 1993*

NERVES AND SOLIDS

THE EIGHTEENTH CENTURY'S most influential tract on farming is *Observations In Husbandry* by Hampshire gentleman farmer Edward Lisle (1666–1722).

Lisle travelled around England's farms taking endless notes. But he died before he could publish his writings and they were eventually printed thirty-five years after his death.

Lisle recommended a farming career on the basis that it was good for the health: 'The nerves and all the solids of the farmers' and labourers' bodies are much stronger than those of gentlemen, who live an idle and unactive life. ... Ordinary medicines work more successfully on their diseases than persons of higher quality. They often arrive at their fulness of years, which gentlemen who are not exercised in country employments, seldom reach. ... Their appetites to their food are much keener, and they receive more nourishment from it than the idle part of mankind would do from the same in quality and quantity. ... I have observed in their death-bed sickness they have kept a found memory and understanding, within a few minutes of their last extremity.'

The greatest danger to the farmer was to catch a heavy cold during freezing weather. Too many farmers went outside without enough warm clothes. Others endangered their health by drinking too much beer. Lisle warned gloomily that such a man would descend into 'a violent sweat, by which the cold has struck so deep as to coagulate the blood and juices, and deaden the tones of all the solids'.

BIRD PULLER

The Roman author and naturalist Pliny the Elder said it was an indication of good soil if crows and other birds followed the ploughman and flocked eagerly to newly turned up earth.

RAINY DAYS

'God made rainy days so gardeners could get the housework done.'

Anon

AN EXTRAVAGANT ORDER OF SLOVENS

AROUND THE TIME OF THE BATTLE OF TRAFALGAR forestry experts were worried that not enough trees were being planted to satisfy the demand for ships' timbers. William Marshall, writing in his 1803 book *On Planting and Rural Ornament: A Practical Treatise*, complained that it was difficult finding foresters who were competent in the art of planting trees.

'A slovenly planter ranks among the most extravagant order of slovens', Marshall grumbled. 'The labour, the plants and the ground are thrown away to the disgrace not only to the individual but to the art itself. When we consider the prodigious quantity of timber which is consumed in the construction of a large vessel we feel a concern for the probable situation of this country at some future period.'

A 74-gun ship, the mainstay of the world's naval fleets, swallowed up two thousand mature oak trees grown on about fifty acres of woodland. Marshall added: 'When we consider the number of king's ships that have been built during the late wars, and the East Indiamen merchants ships, colliers and small craft that are launched daily in the different ports of the kingdom we are ready to tremble for the consequences.' As it happened, Marshall's worries about timber shortages were to have little consequence in the coming age of steel and with the commissioning of the Royal Navy's first iron-clad frigate in 1843.

BEECH OF A HEADACHE

THE STRANGEST OLD ENGLISH COUNTRY LIQUEUR is gin flavoured with beech leaves. Known as beech leaf noyau the drink is believed to have originated in the Chilterns, where there are large areas of beech woods. Connoisseurs admire its potent and distinctive tang.

Gather very young, velvety beech tree leaves stripped from the stem. Add to a jar and cover with a bottle of gin. Add a couple of almonds if you like. Stopper the jar and store for three weeks before straining. Make a sweet syrup from sugar and water and blend it with the spirit. Sharpen with 200ml brandy. Keep for as long as you like. Drink neat, as a mixer, or over ice. (At the Duke of Norfolk's Arundel estate they drink it at the end of shoot lunches.)

• You can also make hawthorn noyau by using the same recipe but with hawthorn buds.

FISHING IN THE WIND

THE LAST TRUE COUNTRYMAN TO LEAD BRITAIN was the late Sir Alec Douglas-Home, Prime Minister for only one year from 1963 to 1964.

Sir Alec (1903–1995) was brought up on the Scottish family estate at the Hirsel in Berwickshire. His father, the 13th Earl of Home, was determined to instil a sense of all things rural in his sons. Thus the moment the Home boys could walk they were taken outside every morning to see from which direction the wind was blowing.

'It mattered a lot', Sir Alec recalled in his 1976 autobiography, aptly titled *The Way The Wind Blows*. 'When the wind blew icy from the north, my father would take us to find the woodcock hidden under evergreen, juniper, holly, yew or rhododendron, besides the springs which never froze. When the wind blew from the west, we would go down to an embankment running along the River Tweed, which was built by French prisoners after the Napoleonic war. … There we would lie at dusk and my father would tell us that we need not be really alert until the first star could be seen in the sky, and the green plovers came flopping over, for they always preceded the ducks in the evening flight. I had the keener eyes, and my brother Henry the quicker ears. We could at an early age identify all the birds in the Border country by sight or sound. I can still remember the almost suffocating excitement of seeing a Roseate starling sitting on the lawn a few yards outside our drawing room.'

Sir Alec, later a life peer as Lord Home of the Hirsel, remembered a most extraordinary day's fishing on the Tweed on 13th November 1926 when he was aged 23: 'I had anticipated, from my knowledge of which way the wind blew that the conditions would be ideal for a few hours, and that thereafter the river would rise quickly into a flood.' He reached the river at 7 a.m. as it became light. By midday he had caught no fewer than nine salmon averaging just under twenty pounds each.

SYMBOL OF CIVILISATION

'The plough remains the symbol of civilisation, for it enables man to cease his nomadic life and become a settler and a builder ... it was the instrument by which he fulfilled the divine command to subdue the earth.'

Landowner, rural writer and organic farming pioneer
Rolf Gardiner (1902–1971)

GOOD SHAPE

How to prune a rose:

- Prune in autumn or spring in order to keep roses in shape and to encourage more flower growth and healthy plants.

- Remove dead shoots and the tips of stems showing signs of dying back.

- Look for crossing and badly placed branches and cut them out to form a good shape.

- Cut the stems of hybrid tea roses to half their length. Floribunda roses can be cut back further. Cut just above a bud pointing in the direction you want the new growth.

- Avoid spreading disease by making sure your secateurs are clean and sharp.

- Always try to prune when the rose is dormant, after autumn leaf fall and before the buds break in spring.

Gardeners' World *Magazine*

RAT-CATCHER

A SPLENDID DESCRIPTION of a rat-catcher by Victorian sporting writer Charles White:

'The destruction of the rat, if it may be called a sport, is certainly the lowest in this country. In other diversions, the killing of the object pursued is generally followed by the cooking of a good dish, or securing the fur for some useful purpose. Hence the rat-catcher comes under the denomination of a man employed to abate a nuisance. The fox, it is true, is not cooked: but Reynard, although a very great destroyer of game and poultry, affords that healthful exercise in the chase which is, in itself, a sufficient recompense. The rat-catcher was formerly distinguished by wearing a broad belt, similar to a sword-belt, which was usually painted blue, and on it were figured a number of the "varmint", in various attitudes. He had, also, other significant emblems of his trade about him, and generally held in his hand a wire cage, and was accompanied, on all occasions, by his dogs. This costume is not now so common as it was some years since. The genuine rat-catcher is an experienced hand in his way. He employs the best terrier dogs, from the wire-haired Scotch breed to the smooth, milk-white species: he uses poison as occasion serves, is dexterous in setting the trap, and extremely clever in the management of the ferret.'

Charles White, Sporting Scenes and Country Characters, *published 1840*

UNLUCKY DOG

Rural superstition decrees that pulling up mandrake is unlucky. To get round this you should tie a dog by its lead to the mandrake root and then tempt it with a bit of meat so it runs towards you and pulls the root out. Mandrake root has been used since ancient times as an anaesthetic.

SUNNIEST

The sunniest place in Great Britain is the Isle of Wight,
where residents enjoy an average of 37.4 hours
of sunshine a week.

SUN-STAINED FLUSH

'WHAT FRUIT CAN COMPARE WITH THE APPLE for its extended
season, lasting from August to June, keeping alive for us in winter, in its sun-stained flush and rustic russet, the memory of golden autumnal days? Through
all the seven ages of man it finds a welcome, and we now learn that not only
does it keep the doctor from our house but ourselves from the dentist. Is there
any other edible which is at once an insurance, a pleasure, and an economy?'

An example of the charming, upper-class camp writing style of Kentish
pomologist Edward 'Bunny' Bunyard (1878–1939), whose classic 1929 book
The Anatomy of Dessert has been described as a 'fetishistic handbook of fruit
exaltation' that encompasses 'all the temperate fruits that could be enjoyed at
the grand finale of dinner – the fresh fruit dessert'.

• The number of UK orchards has fallen by 75 per cent since 1950.

TEST

'The test of a river is its power to drown a man.'

Old fisherman's saying

LUXURY FOR THE POOR

In the mid-1800s over a hundred and fifty named varieties of gooseberries were grown in Britain, notably in Lancashire where the weavers were expert at creating hybrid varieties of gooseberry plants. Gooseberries were known in Victorian times as 'luxury for the poor' because they could be grown in tiny back gardens and were relatively tasty when compared to the space they needed to flourish.

Gooseberry juice has long been known as a treatment for dandruff. Mix with almond oil and massage into the scalp.

POTHOLE

How to fill in a pothole in a gravel drive:

1. Rake or shovel out any loose stones, gravel or soil from the bottom of the pothole.
2. If the sides of the pothole are loose, cut them straight down with a shovel to create firm edges.
3. Fill the hole with coarse gravel to about three inches below the level of the driveway.
4. Tamp down the gravel with a wooden tamping tool constructed from a small square of ¾-inch plywood nailed to the bottom end of a four-foot length of two-by-four.
5. Fill the last three inches with gravel that matches the driveway. Mound it just above the surface.
6. Run a wheel of your car over the spot a few times to compact it down.

• Avoid the contractor who knocks on your door and tells you that he can resurface your drive very cheaply because he has a 'bit of tarmac left over from a job we have been doing for the council'. Bitter experience suggests that he is most likely lying and will almost certainly rip you off. Likewise, the contractor who says he will fill your pot-holes with tarmac 'left over from another job' thereby implying that he is saving you money (which he most definitely isn't), will probably be using a cold asphalt repair product that can be bought from most builders' merchants.

THREE KILLERS

'There are only three things that can kill a farmer: lightning, rolling over in a tractor, and old age.'

American Anglophile author Bill Bryson

HOP FACTS

IN A HOP GARDEN you have eighty-four rows of poles to fourteen acres of ground. Wires are stretched between the poles. From the wires hang lengths of thick coconut string, up which climb the hop plants, known as heels. The wires last for years but it is said that when one goes they all go. Up to 30,000 miles of string are used each year in Kent alone.

FOOLS

I think that I shall never see
A poem lovely as a tree.
A tree whose hungry mouth is prest
Against the sweet earth's flowing breast;
A tree that looks at God all day,
And lifts her leafy arms to pray;
A tree that may in summer wear
A nest of robins in her hair;
Upon whose bosom snow has lain;
Who intimately lives with rain.
Poems are made by fools like me,
But only God can make a tree.

'Trees', *by American poet Joyce Kilmer*
(1886–1918)

MONSTER MOUSE

THE COUNTRYSIDE'S PUBLIC ENEMY NO. 1 is the edible (or fat) dormouse, a tubby rodent-vandal of up to seven inches long, with a thick bushy tail and a lifespan of up to nine years.

The creature was accidentally introduced into Britain at the beginning of the nineteenth century by banker and zoologist Walter, 2nd Baron Rothschild. Trouble began when a couple escaped from Rothschild's private zoo at Tring Park, Hertfordshire.

By 2010 the edible dormouse was top of a list of the most destructive foreign animals in the UK. Despite looking cute and cuddly, it can wreck woodland by stripping bark from trees. It likes to munch through fruit crops such as apples and plums and is partial to domestic electric wiring. Unlike its distant cousin, the native English hazel dormouse, the edible version is far from endangered: there are around 30,000 in the UK.

Other species on the dangerous list include the grey squirrel, the American mink (which has devastated Britain's native water voles), the red-necked wallaby and the muntjac deer. Wallabies threaten Scotland's capercaillie population and muntjac cause hideous damage to crops.

• The dormouse is not really a mouse at all, but a rodent that is closer to a squirrel. It is distinguished by a furry, rather than scaly, tail. The common British mouse is a completely different animal, of which there are five species to be found in the United Kingdom: the harvest mouse, house mouse, wood mouse, field mouse and yellow-necked mouse.

• It is perfectly legal to shoot and eat edible dormice. In case you do, here is a recipe for pan-fried dormice:

Skin and gut four dormice and flour them all over. Fry the dormice in a little oil until browned. Scald two potatoes unpeeled in boiling water, then peel and quarter them. Add potatoes to the dormouse pan and cook briefly. Transfer to a saucepan and de-glaze the pan with water and a little wine. You should have about ¾ pint of liquid. Pour the liquid over the mice and potatoes. Add some lemon peel and simmer slowly until the potatoes break up. Sprinkle with a little wine vinegar before serving.

• Note! It is completely illegal to disturb, harm or kill a common, or hazel, dormouse. Their population has plummeted by 70 per cent since the 1980s and you have to take a dormouse handling course before you're allowed near one. The penalty for even *disturbing* a dormouse is probably worse than if you had killed your granny.

SODDING LAWNS

If you hear a groundsman refer to 'sodding lawns' he is not complaining about the state of the grass, but using a quaint Edwardian expression concerning the laying of turf.

WOODCOCK WONDER

OBSCURE 1810 RECIPE for 'eborised' woodcock:

'Cut into pieces two half roasted woodcocks and put them into a saucepan with three quarters of a pint of gravy, an onion stuck with a few cloves, some pickled mushrooms, a small anchovy, a piece of butter rolled in flour, a blade of mace, and white pepper and salt to the taste. Simmer for about fifteen minutes (do not boil) and then add a quarter of a pint of red wine. Serve hot.'

LE LIGHT BULB

Q: How many French farmers does it take to change a light bulb?

A: Three. Farmer 1 buys a new light bulb. Farmer 2 notices that it has been imported from Britain and promptly sets fire to it. Farmer 1 has to go and get another light bulb. By now Farmer 2 has gone on strike so Farmer 3 has to be brought in to change it.

AL FRISKY

ONE OF THE MORE EARTHY COUNTRY SPORTS to gain popularity in twenty-first century Britain is the sexual practice of dogging, which involves couples having it off in cars in front of strangers in remote rural locations.

The internet has created a dogging boom, with endless lists of suitable trysting places around the country. Secluded car parks, beauty spots, viewpoints etc. are all fair game for a round of jig-a-jig in the Ford Focus.

'Dogging involves exhibitionism and voyeurism', according to one website. 'The voyeurs are mainly men and the exhibitionists are mainly couples or women who love to attract attention and often invite people to join in.

'Experienced doggers communicate their intentions with signals. But don't sneak up on unsuspecting folks. Not every parked couple is looking for attention, so approach with caution. Leaving the interior car light on means they want to be watched. A rolled down window is an invitation to get closer. But make sure the couple is actually dogging; they may have just dropped the keys on the floor or need fresh air. Most importantly, be appreciative but respectful. No hooting, catcalling, or yelling, "Show us yer tits"!'

- The term 'dogging' dates from the early seventies, when a Peeping Tom would 'dog' a couple's every move in order to watch them.

- A 2003 survey by Shropshire agricultural college, Harper Adams, of 260 country parks found that 60 per cent recorded an increase in outdoor sexual activity, including dogging. Warning: dogging can be dangerous and couples have been subjected to robbery and even blackmail. Participants are advised to make sure they are not followed home.

- The act of having sex in a parked car is known as amomaxia (etymology uncertain).

- Dogging should not be confused with 'dogging in', which keen shots will know means using gundogs to drives game birds back into covert to prevent them wandering off. Wives should note that when your husband says he is going dogging in, it does not mean he's up to monkey business in the Range Rover …

MANLIKE WOMAN

The first work on fly-fishing was written by a woman, Juliana Berners, prioress of the nunnery of Sopwell, north of London, who in 1496 produced an essay called the 'Treatyse of Fysshynge wyth an Angle'.

Juliana was a noblewoman well versed in field sports of all kinds. A historian subsequently described her as 'a manlike woman endowed with brilliant gifts of nature'. She is credited with establishing fishing as a proper sport alongside hunting. Her most significant contribution to fly fishing is her description of twelve fly patterns and the months in which they should be used.

'Fysshynge' describes how angling was practised in mid-fifteenth century England. Berners is believed to have done her fishing, mainly for trout, on the chalk stream of the River Ver in Hertfordshire. She used a revolutionary three-piece rod, around eighteen feet long: a six-foot butt of hazel, ash or willow was hollowed out so the other two sections, made of blackthorn, crabtree, medlar or juniper, could be stored inside. It was an ingenious instrument for its time.

The hook was fashioned from a needle; the line was horsehair. Juliana included in her book a list of fish and advice on how many hairs – i.e. how heavy a line – was needed to catch them. Minnows required one hair, and salmon fifteen. There were instructions for dyeing the hair, with colours for different conditions – green for summer, yellow for autumn, russet for winter, black for slow waters and tawny for marshy waters. However, the fly reel would not be invented for another sixty years so the fifteenth-century fisherman had to be content with a fixed length of line.

• Juliana Berners was the first female writer to publish in English.

• The fishing reel first appears in English angling literature in 1651 when it is described as a 'wind' installed within two feet of the lower end of the rod. The Chinese are believed to have used such devices from the twelfth century. Until the 1800s the reel was used as a storage device for excess line: the nineteenth century saw the development of the multiplying reel, which allowed reels to evolve into casting devices – although accomplished anglers also managed surprising distances with well-engineered centrepins.

NORMAL COUNTRYMAN

According to the Duchess of Devonshire, a visitor to Chatsworth wrote in the comments book: 'Saw the Duke in the garden – he looked quite normal.'

SKYGLOW

LIGHT POLLUTION IS THE SCOURGE OF THE COUNTRYSIDE. The last few decades have seen UK light pollution increase at a huge pace.

According to UK government surveys, light pollution has risen by nearly a third since the early 1990s. The West Country has only 20 per cent of dark sky at night left, while Yorkshire and Humberside are down to 11 per cent and the East of England is nearly permanently aglow, with just 5 per cent. The only properly dark places left are in mid-Wales and the Scottish Highlands. Supermarkets and sports grounds are some of the biggest light-polluting culprits in the countryside, but domestic security lighting can be almost as bad.

• Pressure group Environmental Protection UK say that, as well as irritating your neighbours, poorly placed security lighting can have an adverse impact on the behavioural patterns of mammals, birds and fish. To prevent pollution from your security lights you should ask yourself:

- Is lighting necessary?
- Could I achieve the same effect by fencing off a vulnerable area?
- Do lights have to be on all night? If on a PIR, is it working properly?
- For domestic security lights a 150W lamp is adequate. High power (300/500W) lamps create too much glare. For an all-night porch light a 9W lamp is more than adequate.
- Make sure that lights are correctly adjusted so that they only illuminate the surface intended and do not throw light onto neighbouring property.
- To reduce the effects of glare, lights should be angled below 70 degrees.
- If uplighting has to be used then install shields above the lamp to reduce wasted upward light.
- Do not install equipment which spreads light above the horizontal.

• The orange light pollution seen over towns and roads is known as 'skyglow'. As well as looking horrid, this glow is a serious problem for astronomers as the artificial brightness overpowers distant stars.

RURAL CHAT

Topics of conversation at country dinner parties attended by the gentry (courtesy of a selection of the author's friends):

- School fees, outrageous annual increases thereof.

- Asparagus beds.

- Huge, ludicrously expensive lawnmowers, the general unreliability thereof.

- Gutters, always blocked.

- Size of house (far too big but there we go, if it wasn't for that bloody English Heritage I'd knock half of it down).

- Staff – which is better: Polish or indigenous? (Poland wins every time.)

- Pruning box hedges; should it be done on Derby Day?

- Amusing parlour game to see whose house has the most lavatories.

- Shooting.

- Hunting.

- More hunting: who's bonking whom?

- Absurdly low price paid for pheasants by game dealer.

- Latest hunt ball, appalling behaviour witnessed at.

- Yet more assorted adultery, divorce, general shenanigans.

- Range Rovers, on slippery, wet fields, the general uselessness thereof.

- Likewise Discoverys; (old Subarus, can't beat 'em).

- Farm rents.

- Latest outrageously extravagant party by local industrialist to which the gentry were invited: 'He spent *how much* on fireworks?'

- Piss-taking tenantry who are paying ludicrously low rents thanks to the Agricultural Holdings Act.

- Tricky gamekeepers who refuse to double up as gardeners.

- Central heating oil, exorbitant cost thereof.

- Bats and newts and any other mammals, amphibians, which hold up residential barn conversions: 'If I had my way I'd shoot/depth charge the lot of 'em.'

- Wood-burning stoves: 'absolutely marvellous darling, never been so warm'.

- Time it takes to get to London (women only, as the men never want to go anywhere).

- Mansion tax: 'This place is so big it will cost me fifty grand a year, ho, ho.'

- Badgers and bovine TB; disgraceful back-tracking on a cull by cowardly Conservative ministers.

- General aversion to Liberal Democrats: 'I'd rather have a Labour chap sitting next to me at dinner any day.'

KEEPING TRACK

Anyone who has had to fill in government farming forms will know how hard it is to keep track of the different acronyms used by the Department of Environment, Food and Rural Affairs (Defra). Here are a few to help you get through the paperwork:

CPH County Parish Holding

CSS Countryside Stewardship Scheme

ERDP England Rural Development Programme

ESA Environmentally Sensitive Area

FDS Farm Diversification Scheme

FEP Farm Environment Plan

FER Farm Environmental Record

FVP Fruit – Vegetables – Potatoes

FWAG Farming and Wildlife Advisory Group

FWPS Farm Woodlands Premium Scheme

FYM Farm Yard Manure

GAEC Good Agricultural and Environmental Condition

HER Historic Environment Records

IACS Integrated Administration and Control System

LFA Less Favoured Area

LU Livestock Unit

NVZ Nitrate Vulnerable Zones

OAS Organic Aid Scheme

OELS Organic Entry Level Stewardship

OFS Organic Farming Scheme

PCP Protein Crop Premium

RLR Rural Land Register

SBI Single Business Identifier

SDA Severely Disadvantaged Area

SRC Short Rotation Coppice

SPARKY

Advice from *The Field Book of Country Queries* (1989) on how to prevent sparky logs when burning coniferous wood: 'These woods contain small knots … which "pop" under heat. The simplest way to check the sparking is to sprinkle salt lightly on the logs when they have begun to burn and repeat when fresh logs are added. It helps if the logs are cut in small, chunky pieces and are added with the bark facing inwards. Feed a wood fire from the back, placing fresh logs more or less behind those already burning.'

• Folklore dictates that if you poke the fire and it burns brightly, your sweetheart is in a good temper.

SILAGE STUFF

G RASS SILAGE forms the main winter feed for cattle throughout Britain. Approximately 38 million tons of pickled grass is made each year in the UK. Most silage is collected and put into silage clamps. Around 17 per cent is made in big plastic bales of the type that you see littering the countryside from early summer.

Silage is fermented, high-moisture fodder that can be fed to cud-chewing animals such as cows and sheep. Everything from maize to alfalfa can be used, though in Britain it is created mainly from grass.

The pasture must be cut when the grasses contain their highest nutrient levels. This usually happens just before they are fully mature. All forms of preserved grass, such as hay and silage, will have lower amounts of nutrients than fresh pasture, so everything must be done to make the end product as nutritious as possible.

Cut grass is allowed to wilt in the field for a few hours to reduce the moisture content to around 60–75 per cent. This will allow for optimum fermentation. If the grass is left out longer, it may get too dry, or rained on, and both these conditions will reduce proper fermentation. The longer the grass is left uncut, the higher the loss of nutrients. It is important that the cut grass is compacted to release as much oxygen as possible: the bacteria needed to carry out the fermentation prefer an oxygen-free environment.

• The only celebrity to have been killed by silage was Michael Edwards, founder member of the rock group Electric Light Orchestra. Edwards, a cellist, died in 2010 when a 400-kilogram bale of silage rolled down a steep field onto his car as he drove along a rural Devon road.

UPON THE CURLING SURFACE

EIGHTEENTH-CENTURY ANGLER Thomas Best presents his Top 10 rules for the perfect day's fly fishing:

1. The best fishing is in a river somewhat disturbed with rain, or on a cloudy day, when the waters are moved with a gentle breeze: the south and west winds are the best: and if the wind blows high, yet not so but that you may conveniently guide your tackle, the fishes will rise in the still deeps; but if there is little wind stirring, the best angling is in swift streams.

2. In casting your line, do it always before you, and in such a manner that the fly may fall first on the water, and as little of your line with it as possible; but if the wind is high, you will then be forced to drown a good part of it, that you may keep the fly on the water. Endeavour to have the wind at your back, and the sun in your face.

3. When you throw your line, wave the rod in a small circumference round your head, and never make a return of it before it has had its full scope – for if you do the fly will snap off.

4. Although when you angle the day is cloudy and windy, and the water thick, you must keep the fly in continual motion, otherwise the fishes will discern the deceit.

5. Let the line be twice as long as the rod, unless the river is encumbered with wood; and always stand as far off the bank as the length of your line will permit, when you cast the fly to the contrary side; but if the wind blows so that you must throw your line on the same side you are on, stand on the very brink of the river, and cast your fly at the utmost length of the rod and line, tip or down the stream as the wind serves.

6. You must have a quick sharp eye, and active hand, to strike directly a fish rises; or else, finding the mistake, he will spew out the hook.

7. Small light coloured flies are for clear waters, and clear atmospheres, large dark coloured flies when vice versa.

8. When after rain the water becomes brownish, an orange coloured fly is taken greedily. When fishes rise at the fly very often, and yet never take it, you may conclude that it is not what they like; therefore change it for one they do.

9. When you see a fish rise, throw your fly beyond him, and draw it gently over the place, where he rose; and if it is a proper fly for the season, and you cast it with a nicety, the fish is your own. When you angle in slow running rivers, or still places, with an artificial fly, cast it across the water, and let it sink a little in the water, and then draw it gently over to you again, letting the current carry it slowly down. This is the best way for slow waters; but for quick ones your fly must always swim on the top, under the continual inspection of your eyes. It is a good plan always to carry some dubbing, gut, hooks, and silk, out with you in a small pocket-book, that you may be able always to imitate any fly you see the fish rise at more than others.

10. The lighter your flies fall on the water the better; this you will not accomplish by strength, but by practice, always raising your rod by degrees, after you have made your cast. A young angler should never use more than one fly on the stretcher at first, but when he can throw out pretty well, he may add to the stretcher one or more droppers, observing always to let them be one yard asunder.

From A Concise Treatise on the Art of Angling, *by Thomas Best, 1787*

RURAL TIP

'If you are walking with a woman in the country, ascending a mountain or strolling by the bank of a river, and your companion being fatigued, should choose to sit upon the ground, on no account allow yourself to do the same, but remain rigorously standing. To do otherwise would be flagrantly indecorous and she would probably resent it as the greatest insult.'

From Decorum: A Practical Treatise on Etiquette,
J.A. Ruth & Co., 1877

BASTARDS

Top 10 items likely to be found illegally fly-tipped in the countryside, according to the Environment Agency:

1. Bin bags of household rubbish
2. Garden waste
3. Timber and fencing
4. Builders' rubble
5. Window frames
6. Tyres
7. Asbestos
8. Calor gas bottles
9. Retail waste
10. Carpets, beds and bedding

• Fly-tipping is an arrestable offence. The maximum penalty under the Environmental Protection Act 1990 is an unlimited fine and/or five years in prison. Vehicles used for fly-tipping can be seized.

• Fly-tippers are very difficult to catch, although prosecutions are becoming more frequent. In 2009–10 in England and Wales there were nearly 947,000 fly-tipping incidents resulting in 2,374 successful prosecutions.

• Fly-tipping on agricultural land costs private landowners around £100 million per annum to clear.

• Fly-tipping reached new heights in 2006 when litter-pickers doing a clean-up on the 4,418ft summit of Ben Nevis in the Scottish Highlands found an upright piano hidden under some rocks. It was believed that someone must have hauled it up there as a stunt.

U AND NON-U HORSES

The vexed subject of which horses are U and Non-U is covered here by baronet Sir Andrew Horsburgh-Porter (1907–1986), World War II war hero and 1960s hunting editor of *The Field*:

'The language difficulty is the first obstacle facing the neophyte in the horse and pony world … Even the colour names for ponies sound illogical. One that almost exactly resembles a newly peeled horse-chestnut or 'conker' is described as a bay; while a chestnut horse or pony varies in colour from lemon, through orange marmalade to red, and finally to something like raw liver. The U descriptions of these variations of chestnut are washy, bright, dark and, yes – to make it easy, liver. A brown horse resembles a glass of Guinness – dark in the body with some tan markings on the extremities – especially on his nose.

Non-U people frequently mistake a brown horse for a black. The body colour is the same, but the black horse has white markings instead of the Guinness-coloured extremities. U horses varying in shade from the colour of untempered steel to white are all grey – it is non-U to call a horse white: the only white horses are those which top the crest of waves on a stormy day at sea. If they have tiny dark spots like measles over their white skin, grey horses are described as flea-bitten, and should this same white skin be covered with odd blotches and whorls of colouring, as if a futuristic Chelsea artist has been at work with a black brush, then dappled grey is their description. Flamboyantly coloured horses – black and white, or spotted, or pale yellow like golden coins – are popular, but only in the last few years have they ceased to be connected with the circus. There is now a Palomino society – Palominos are the pale yellow ones – and all societies are U.'

From 'What Are U', a collection of writings on class, edited by Alan Ross, published by Andre Deutsch Ltd, 1969

USUALLY MEANS RAIN

Some tips on amateur weather forecasting by seventeenth-century Hampshire squire John Worlidge, taken from his popular 1699 book *Systema Agriculturae*:

If small black clouds appear on a clear evening, it means rain.

If on a good day the sky is dappled with white clouds (a so-called mackerel sky) it usually means rain.

If during a cold, dry winter's day great black clouds come from the north and appear whitish when near to you, it signifies snow or hail.

If small waterish clouds appear on the tops of hills, rain follows. Typical to Cornwall.

Clouds moving towards the sun denote high winds.

If clouds rest over the sun at sunrise, looking a little like an eclipse, it portends wind.

If while the rain is lashing down the winds rise or fall, it signifies that the rain will stop.

If at the beginning of the winter the south wind blows, and then the north, it is like to be a cold winter. But if the north wind blows first, and then the south, it will be a warm and mild winter.

FERRET ADVICE

'Ferrets that are kept for rabbiting should never be used to hunt rats. A rabbit ferret that has been set ratting is almost sure to be badly bitten by the rats, and this makes him nervous, and vicious, and dangerous to handle. He is likely to bite you when you put your hand in a rabbit's hole. I could pull a properly trained ferret out of the hole by his fore-foot, tail, loins, or even by his under jaw, and he would never bite me, but I never attempted to take liberties with a ratting ferret.'

John Wilkins,
The Autobiography of an English Gamekeeper, *1892*

TOTALLY NUTS

Architectural history author Sir Nikolaus Pevsner (1902–1983), who spent years travelling round Britain's stately homes researching his *Buildings Of England* series, dedicated his 1968 volume on Bedfordshire to 'the inventor of the ice lolly'.

Pevsner spent so much of his time on the road that he became an expert in fast food such as fish 'n' chips as well as all types of ice cream cone and lolly. His favourite lunch was a week-old camembert sandwich. Pevsner complained later, 'The journeys are just not human'. When asked if he would update the books at some stage, he replied, 'They will need somebody else who is totally nuts to do it again.'

Pevsner's unique inventory of English buildings comprises 20,000 pages in forty-six volumes. The series has been universally acclaimed as the result of a combination of scholarship and a cast-iron stomach.

• Nikolaus Pevsner would have known that the ice lolly was invented by an American called Frank Epperson who began selling his 'Epsicles' in 1922. He later changed the name to Popsicle.

LAMBY LAB

Britain's greatest road kill connoisseur is Arthur Boyt from Cornwall, a retired civil servant in his sixties. Mr Boyt has spent years scraping dead animals off roads before cooking them. He has tried everything from weasels and rats to cats and dogs – notably a Labrador which he found without a collar: 'There was nothing to show who its owner was even though it was in good condition. I took it home and ate it. It was like a nice piece of lamb.' His most unusual find was a greater horseshoe bat: 'It tastes similar to grey squirrel.' He has tried otter and once tucked into a porcupine while on holiday in Canada.

Mr Boyt insists that road kill is not a health risk if butchered and cooked properly: 'It's good meat for free and I know nobody has been messing with it and feeding it hormones.' He argues that people should no more recoil at the idea of road kill than object to an apple that has fallen from a tree.

WOULD RATHER HAVE MEASLES

In seventeenth century England it was thought that measles could be cured by drinking tea made from sheep droppings.

FOR A RAINY DAY

How to make a milking stool:

'A thick slab of wood makes the seat. Elm is best because it resists splitting and warping. You also need three turned legs. Use a saw to convert the slab into a disc and then round off the edges. Gouge out the centre of the seat to form a comfortable depression. Mark the positions for the legs: set the point of a compass on the rim, adjust it to a radius equal to that of the seat and mark the two points where the compass line meets the rim; set the compass on them to mark more points and so on – you will end up with six points marked. Divide the disc into thirds by drawing a radius to every alternate point from the centre: these are the lines along which to set the three legs, at about three inches from the edge of the seat. They will be splayed rather than vertical so you need to drill holes for them at a slight angle. Make the holes all the way through the thickness of the seat and slightly

smaller than the leg diameter. Little by little, taper the tops of the legs slightly so that they can be pushed into the holes with their tops flush with the top of the seat and no further. When you have achieved a good 'push fit', remove them and cut out a notch in the tapered end before pushing them back into place, then tamp wedges into the notches from above to expand the leg across the grain of the seat – you can add glue to the wedges for good measure. Trim off any wedge protrusions so that the seat is flush and trim off the ends of the legs so that the stool stands square to the floor.'

Note: a three-legged milking stool should have one leg slightly longer than the other two so that it slopes forward slightly, making it more comfortable for the milkmaid.

From Cottage Industries, Information For Beginners, *by Valerie Porter, published by Swan Hill Press, 1992*

GOOD STURDY LAD

Excerpt from a letter by nineteenth-century countryside campaigner William Cobbett to a friend requesting help to find him the perfect farm lad:

'I want neither science nor advice. I want legs that will move nimbly and willingly, and a young head capable of learning. The lad ought to be stout, and not stunted; he ought to be able to read and write a little; but, two things are indispensable; namely, that his father be a farmer, and that the son has lived on a farm in England all his life. ... He is to sit at table with my brother and my niece (who is the housekeeper), and me. He is never to quit the farm except to go to the parish church on the Sunday. He will here learn all about cultivation of Indian Corn, Mangel Wurzle. ... He will learn to sow and rear trees, and to plant and prune them. ... If the lad stay a year out, I will make him a present of not less than ten or twelve guineas. It is, I hope, unnecessary to add that this is a farm house without a tea kettle or a coffee pot and without any of the sweets that come from the sweats of African slaves. Please to observe, that I do not want a young gentleman, but a good sturdy lad whose hands do not instinctively recoil from a frozen chain, or from the dirty heels of an ox or a horse. I hope that the lad will never have been at an establishment, vulgarly called a boarding school: if he unfortunately have, I must sweat the boarding-school nonsense out of him.'

• Cobbett (1763–1835) is described as 'the most vocal representative of peasant England in its latter days'. He is best known for his 1830 book *Rural Rides*, which describes his journeys through south-east England and the Midlands.

• Cobbett observed country life from the view of both farmer and social reformer. He wrote, 'In all the really agricultural villages and parts of the kingdom there is shocking decay; a great dilapidation and constant pulling down or falling down of houses.'

PLEASING

'Though every prospect pleases,
And only man is vile.'

Reginald Heber, Bishop of Calcutta (1783–1826). Heber's famous lines are frequently used to describe how man has helped to destroy the countryside. They appear in his 1819 missionary hymn *From Greenland's Icy Mountains*.

BIG FISH

THE BIGGEST PIKE caught in the British Isles is widely accepted as being a fifty-three-pounder hooked on Lough Conn in Ireland in 1920, although this is no longer accepted as the official record because the tests and checks required for verification nowadays were not in place at that time. Continental pike can be even bigger. In 1862 a beast weighing 145 pounds was caught at Bregenz, Austria.

STUPID HAT

Top 10 tips for staying warm as you rattle around in the draughty old pile complaining about the ridiculous cost of heating oil:

1. Dress in layers, the more the better. Layers trap the warm air better and are much more efficient than grandfather's moth-eaten old trench coat.

2. Wool will keep you warm even when it is wet. No synthetic material will do this.

3. Natural materials breathe better, crucial when you work up a sweat and need to evaporate it so you don't get cold when you slow down.

4. The warmest outer garment you can find is a down coat.

5. A pair of wool gloves covered by a second layer of synthetic mittens is the best way of keeping your hands warm.

6. Don't let your brain get cold! Just because your head does not feel cold it does not mean you are not losing heat from the top of your head. Loss of heat from the head will make your feet and hands cold.

7. It is said that the more stupid your hat looks (i.e. leather covered, sheepskin ear muffs), the warmer it is.

8. Wear wool socks and insulated boots to keep your feet warm.

9. Keep your neck warm with a scarf. This seals the top of your jacket so that warm air does not leak out. You can lose a lot of heat this way. Likewise make sure your jacket cuffs are sealed.

10. If the rest of your body is warm, you can afford to lose warmth through your face meaning that you don't have to cover it up with an uncomfortable balaclava or suchlike.

SUPERSTITIOUS

There are numerous variations of the magpie rhyme but one of the most common is:

One for sorrow
Two for joy
Three for a girl
Four for a boy
Five for silver
Six for gold
Seven for a secret never to be told
Eight for a lie
Nine for a truth
Ten for the secret of eternal youth.

Note: to mitigate the bad luck a single magpie brings it should be greeted with a low bow. You can also repeat the words, 'I defy thee', seven times.

During the Napoleonic Wars the rhyme was altered to:

One for sorrow
Two for mirth
Three for a wedding
Four for death
Five for a fiddle
Six for a dance,
Seven for England
Eight for France.

• 'A single magpie in spring, foul weather will bring.' This superstition arises from the fact that pairs of magpies tend to forage together only when the weather is fine.

• In Northamptonshire three magpies signify a fire.

• Lincolnshire folk would cross themselves if they saw a magpie.

• Devon peasantry would spit over their shoulder three times if they saw a magpie.

• The boys in Biggar, Scotland, believed that if you cut a magpie's tongue with a crooked sixpence it would speak like a human being. Who on earth dreamed up that one?

FIGHT BACK

Residents in the tiny York village of Draughton decided to fight back against the decline in rural services in 2010 by opening a grocery store in a disused telephone box. A newsagent from nearby Skipton supplied the box with basic provisions such as bread, milk, jam, tea bags and newspapers. Based on the 'honesty box' principle, residents left payment for any goods they took.

VERY DANGEROUS

BRITAIN'S QUIRKIEST RURAL CONTEST is the annual World Stone Skimming Championships at Easdale Island, near Oban in Argyll, Scotland. In late September each year hundreds of people descend on Easdale, the smallest permanently inhabited island of the Inner Hebrides. Anyone can enter using special Easdale slate skimming stones no more than three inches across. For a skim to qualify the stone must bounce at least three times and stay within a designated lane marked by buoys. It is judged on the distance achieved before it sinks – skims of well over 230 feet are common place. Entrants over the age of 60 are encouraged to enter the 'Old Tosser' category.

• Stone skimming is better known as 'ducks and drakes'. Prep-school boys of a certain vintage will know that the first rebound of the pebble after striking the surface of the water is termed a 'dick', the second a 'duck', and the third a 'drake'. Aficionados of this pastime say that pieces of broken tiles make the best skimmers and can achieve up to ten bounces.

• The only person thought to have died while playing ducks and drakes is 17-year-old Irishman Nelson Bell who, in 1887, expired after being struck on the head with a pebble while skimming stones with friends on a pond at Ballymacbrennan, County Down. Passing a verdict of accidental death, the foreman of the inquest jury, Mr Andrew Gillespie, noted that ducks and drakes was 'a very dangerous game'. One for the health 'n' safety police?

GLOWING FOLIAGE

Top 10 plants for autumn colour:

1. *Vitis coignetiae* (Japanese crimson glory vine). Can reach a height of 85 feet; a display of crimson, purple, yellow and orangey-red.

2. *Cotinus* (smoke bush). Glowing foliage in several different colours.

3. *Rosa moyesii* ('geranium') produces displays of bright orange flask-shaped hips. Does best in full sun.

4. *Aesculus parviflora*. Related to the conker tree, but small enough for a garden. Rich yellow foliage; best in sheltered sites.

5. Cotoneasters, such as *C. lacteus* and *C. conspicuus* 'decorus', have brilliant red berries.

6. *Euonymus europaeus* (red cascade), a relative of the spindle bush, has tiny but impressive fruits, Does well on chalk.

7. *Callicarpa bodinieri*, especially 'profusion', looks as if the stems have had clumps of bright, often purple, polystyrene balls stuck on.

8. *Cercidiphyllum japonicum*. In autumn the rounded leaves of this tree turn various shades of red and gold.

9. *Fothergilla major* and *F. gardenii*. Both these shrubs offer fantastic yellow, gold, orange and rich red autumn foliage; delicately perfumed white flowers in spring.

10. *Viburnum opulus* or guelder rose has translucent red berries in autumn. The foliage also turns an attractive yellow.

PYLON PAINTING

'Painters of the rural scene in the 20th century have been notorious for their inability to see pylons and silage towers. "Discussing the Milk Quota" and "Artificial Insemination Day" are still, I believe, subjects awaiting their debut at the Royal Academy.'

W. Vaughan, Leisure and Toil, Differing Views of Rural Life, *1989*

HEDGEHOG TRIVIA

Hedgehogs can kill and eat snakes. Their spines make them immune to attack. Hedgehog blood contains macro-globulins which counter the effects of adder venom.

Hedgehogs eat earthworms, beetles, caterpillars and birds' eggs. Do not feed hedgehogs bread and milk – cow's milk upsets their tummies, although goat's milk is acceptable. Hedgehogs love dog food.

Hedgehogs like solitude. When they are together it is for mating or fighting.

Many hedgehogs drown in garden ponds or swimming pools because they have no way of climbing out. They can catch pneumonia from inhaling water.

Cattle grids should be fitted with ramps so hedgehogs can escape if they tumble in.

During autumn, hedgehogs build winter nests. But they are not streetwise and often choose bonfires for the site. Many get strimmed in long grass in summer.

Hedgehogs get frisky in April. Before mating, the female presses her stomach to the ground and arches her back away from her mate, so that prick does not meet prick, so to speak. Mating hedgehogs are very noisy.

The hedgehog's big enemy is the badger, one of the few predators which has learned to unroll a hedgehog and bite into its underbelly.

Historically, hedgehogs were usually considered pests. Church wardens would pay twopence for a snout or a tail.

Hedgehogs are an endangered species in Wales, where numbers have been falling dramatically. They are said to have largely disappeared from big cities, including London, thanks to over-manicured gardens. Hedgehogs like scruffy gardens; decking is a nightmare. They are just about holding their own in the English countryside despite threats from pesticides and the removal of hedges. In 1995 there were estimated to be about two million hedgehogs in Britain. By 2011 the figure had halved. If you don't see dead

hedgehogs on the road it is not because they have learned road sense; it is because there are fewer hedgehogs to kill.

> Lily-white and clean, oh!
> With little frills between, oh!
> Smooth and hot – red rusty spot
> Never here be seen, oh!

Beatrix Potter, 1905: Mrs Tiggy-Winkle's song just before she meets Lucie.

Hedgehogs can walk three or four miles in a day.

Hedgehogs can sniff a dog from thirty-five feet away.

A hedgehog can jump two feet to catch a beetle.

A Russian hedgehog once found its way back home after it was dropped forty-eight miles across the tundra.

Hedgehogs should be good at sky-diving. Their spines cushion any fall so that they bounce on landing.

In the 1980s someone produced so-called hedgehog-flavoured crisps with part proceeds going to the British Hedgehog Preservation Society. They tasted like pork sausages.

The 12,000-strong Hedgehog Preservation Society is a formidable pressure group. In 2006 they persuaded fast food giant McDonalds to change the design of the lid on their McFlurry dessert. The original containers were a death trap for hedgehogs who, desperate to get at the remains of the ice cream, would get their heads stuck. The design of the new lid means that even if the cup is discarded with the lid attached, the hole will be too small for hedgehogs to push into.

A hedgehog's first line of defence is to attack. It puts its head down, pushes its spines forwards, gives a loud snort and charges.

A hedgehog will disguise its scent by licking another source of smell such as a dead rabbit and then using its long tongue to cover itself with scented saliva. Sometimes a hedgehog will anoint itself with toxins, such as excretions from a toad's poison gland. This makes the spines poisonous to attackers.

The seventeenth-century philosopher and physician Sir Thomas Browne (1605–1682), propagated the theory that in order to see in the dark all you had to do was eat the right eye of a hedgehog boiled in oil.

Old joke: Q: 'How do hedgehogs make love?'
A: 'Carefully.'

New joke: At the 2009 Edinburgh Festival the best one-liner award went to comic Dan Antopolski for:

'Hedgehogs – why can't they just share the hedge?'

NUTTERS

Until the First World War, Holy Cross Day, 14th September,
was a traditional holiday for children so that they
could go nutting.

THE PROPER PABULUM

Fishing tip:

'I beg the reader to bear in mind that whenever I describe a
favourite, a good, or a general fly, I have this great rule that
large gaudy flies suit only deep and somewhat turbid waters,
and that small, sombre-hued flies are fittest for low and clear
water. Flies of medium size and mediocre brilliancy of colours
are appropriate for water moderately deep and moderately
limpid; and, above all, I tell him who would successfully angle
for salmon, that the weather-glass must be his chief guide. With
mercury falling, no salmon will be seen rising except for
pastime or something of that sort; with mercury rising, salmon
will rise too, not for pastime, but for pasture, if the proper
pabulum be presented to them.'

Edward Fitzgibbon, The Book of the Salmon, *1850*

ACRES OF HAPPINESS

Happy the man, whose wish and care
A few paternal acres bound,
Content to breathe his native air,
In his own ground.

Alexander Pope (1866–1744),
'Ode On Solitude'

THE LOVE OF PROSPECT

THE GEORGIAN LANDSCAPE DESIGNER William Gilpin had a cautionary tale for anyone planning to cut down trees on their estate. In his 1835 book *Practical Hints Upon Landscape Gardening*, he recalled visiting a friend who was building a splendid new house in Oxfordshire.

'It was a knoll covered with full grown wood', Gilpin wrote. 'The openings here and there carried the eye across a valley adorned with the winding reaches of the Thames. Through one of these openings a distant spire was happily, I should rather say unhappily, seen.' Gilpin explained how a visitor had told his friend that if he cut down part of the wood the vista would feature not just one spire but the spires of seven churches.

'In the evil hour he listened to the tempter', Gilpin lamented. And when he next called on his friend he found the wood all but gone and the man 'seated on a bare lawn, contemplating through a telescope his seven churches'. It was, Gilpin said, 'an instance in which the love of prospect has triumphed over taste, comfort, and convenience'.

A CHORUS OF CAR ALARMS

Bird-song notes:

- Birds have either 'calls' that are used to give alarm or maintain contact within a flock in order to find food, or 'songs' which are used to attract mates and defend territories.

- Some species, like gulls and the kingfisher, do not have songs.

- The best example of bird-song is the dawn chorus in the spring and summer. This starts before sunrise with one or two birds, usually the blackbird, followed by the song thrush. Then the robin, wren, great tit and chaffinch join in. More species join in until, by mid-morning, there is a symphony of song.

- The purpose of and reason for the dawn chorus is explained by the fact that the air is cooler at dawn and sound travels further; conditions for searching for food are less favourable around dawn; male birds are guarding their territories and mates from the competition; singing influences the females' reproductive cycle and nest building.

- Mostly male birds sing, though both male and female robins sing during the winter.

- Scientists have worked out that birds are born with a basic singing ability but that they go on to mimic the calls of their parents and other birds they meet along the way.

- A juvenile bird will start to learn to sing with sub-song, or a subdued jumble of notes. Sub-song can be heard during autumn and winter: robins and blackbirds can often be heard singing very quietly, as if to themselves.

- Some species, such as starlings, will also mimic earthly sounds such as car alarms. They will also copy your wolf whistle.

Information courtesy of British Garden Birds, www.garden-birds.co.uk

A GREAT LEVELLER

'GARDENING IS A GREAT LEVELLER. One day you are cock-a-hoop because you have that exquisite *abutilon megapotamicum* in bloom, with its many black, yellow and red Chinese lanterns all glowingly alight; the next you flop hopelessly with pink nerines which you recently saw growing in a cottage garden with all the vigour and freedom of a row of common marigolds. There are plants which love you and plants which don't.'

H.E. Bates, A Love of Flowers, *published by Michael Joseph, 1971*

UNUSED FACULTY

'The tales which pass on the tongues of village people rarely gain or lose in the telling. The plain narrative is told as it was heard. After twenty minds have taken it in and given it out again it remains almost the same. Much of the gossip is "news", which usually moves in a circular path, returning to the subject of it.'

Henry Williamson, The Village Book, *published 1930. Williamson, writer on all things rural, is best known for his 1927 best-seller* Tarka the Otter.

NEVER EVER ...

SHOOTING was well covered in my book *The Keen Shot's Miscellany*. However, so many people are learning to shoot game these days that one cannot give enough lectures about gun safety. Here are some vital tips that were given in the 1960s and are as relevant as ever today:

1. Break a gun and prove whether or not it is loaded as soon as you lay hands on it.
2. Never point a gun at anyone.
3. Learn to shoot in good style; good shooting promotes safe shooting.
4. Check that the bore of your gun is clear before you load it at the beginning of a day, shoot drive or walk-up or any other interval between shooting. [Particularly after a misfire: the author's father narrowly missed blowing himself up when a cartridge misfired and bits of cardboard were left in the barrel.]
5. Never put down or leave a loaded gun.
6. Always carry your gun safely, with the barrels pointing either up in the air or down at the ground, except when you come to the ready position prior to taking a shot, when they should point where you are looking.
7. Don't shoot where you cannot see; shot can travel up to three hundred yards and rifle bullets much further.
8. Always unload your gun when crossing a hedge, fence, ditch, or other obstacle and when entering a car or building.
9. Don't be a greedy shot; greediness leads to taking risks, which leads to dangerous shooting, such as following across the line.
10. Don't take other people blindly on trust as safe shots. [Too true – author.]

From Gun Safety *by Roderick Willett, published by Arlington Books, 1967*

GORGEOUS

'It is the best cheese that England affords, if not that the whole world affords.'

Daniel Defoe on the subject of cheddar, from his 1724 book
Tour Through The Whole Island Of Great Britain

HARD AND LUMPY

A classic Oscar Wilde rant from *Intentions*, a collection of four short works published in 1913:

'But Nature is so uncomfortable. Grass is hard and lumpy and damp, and full of dreadful black insects. … If Nature had been comfortable, mankind would never have invented architecture, and I prefer houses to the open air. In a house we all feel of the proper proportions. Everything is subordinated to us, fashioned for our use and our pleasure. Egotism itself, which is so necessary to a proper sense of human dignity, is entirely the result of indoor life. Out of doors one becomes abstract and impersonal. One's individuality absolutely leaves one. And then Nature is so indifferent, so unappreciative. Whenever I am walking in the park here, I always feel that I am no more to her than the cattle that browse on the slope, or the burdock that blooms in the ditch.'

PIG SKIN

VICTORIAN DOMESTIC GODDESS Maria Rundel offers a remedy for chapped hands: mix a quarter pound of unsalted hog's lard with rose-water, the yolks of two eggs and a large spoonful of honey. Add oatmeal, work into a paste and cover your hands with it.

BEST SOOT

UNTIL THE END of the 1940s chimney soot was spread on fields as fertiliser. Soot contained ammonia salts which made it nitrogenous manure. The rule was, the lighter the soot, the higher the nitrogen content and the greater the value.

Soot fertiliser took off in the early 1700s, coinciding with advances in agriculture coupled with a rapid increase in the use of coal fires, particularly in London.

Soot was smelly and endangered health. Yet it was much sought after in the countryside. By the 1780s London chimneys were producing around 20,000 tons of soot per year, the figure doubling by the mid-nineteenth century.

There were three types of soot: the best was produced from pure coal; then came soot from the grates of the poorer classes who mixed coal with potato peelings; finally, there was wood soot, a fairly useless fertiliser nearly ten times heavier than the best.

Farmers used up to half a ton of soot per acre on newly planted cereals. Barley was 'sooted' at the beginning of March. Soil was top-dressed with soot at the end of the year. The most soot was used in the grain belts of Hertfordshire and Bedfordshire because of their proximity to London, while in Scotland, the Earl of Dalhousie's

estate manager Alexander Main invented a machine for spreading soot on grassland. You could tell which sheep had been reared on soot-fertilised grass because their faces were black.

The soot trade suffered a blow in 1842 with the invention of artificial fertiliser, created by John Lawes, an Eton and Oxford-educated Hertfordshire squire. Lawes, aged 26, set up a factory at his family home Rothamsted Manor making what he called 'Superphosphate', composed of phosphate of lime, phosphate of ammonia and silicate of potash. He was honoured with a baronetcy for his efforts. Lawes' legacy lives on at Rothamsted, which his descendants in the 1930s put into trust for crop research. It is still the United Kingdom's largest agricultural research centre.

The soot trade all but died with the introduction of smokeless fuel in the 1950s, though some allotment holders still swear by spreading soot on their vegetable patches.

• Eighteenth-century chimney sweeps often ripped off farmers by adulterating their soot with coal ashes, blacksmith's forge dust and sweepings of burnt cork. A sweep could double his income by operating as a soot dealer.

• The chimneys in some country houses were so vast that the best way to clean them was to tie a rope round the neck of a goose, and drop it squawking and flapping down the chimney so that the action of its wings would dislodge the soot. The blacker the bird, the cleaner the chimney, and the goose would emerge from the fireplace unhurt. A duck worked well on a smaller chimney, while over in Ireland they used turkeys. A heron's wing made a good hearth brush.

• As of 2012 the National Association of Chimney Sweeps has reported a large increase in business thanks to the large number of wood-burning stoves being installed throughout the UK by homeowners desperate to cut fuel bills. Chimneys should be swept after every winter, especially if burning smokeless fuel. Regular sweeping limits damage to the flue caused by acids released when smokeless fuel combusts. This acid can erode the inside of chimneys and make them more likely to catch fire.

CONFUSED

AN AMERICAN AGRICULTURAL WEBSITE explains that you can let people know you are a farmer by using suitably rural expressions such as: 'I'm as nervous as a six-tailed cat in a room full of rocking chairs', or 'I'm more confused than a three-legged pig at a square dance'.

FARMING REVOLUTIONARY

Britain's first big farmer was Thomas Coke (1754–1842). An Old Etonian Norfolk landowner and politician, Coke is credited with sparking the British agricultural revolution through the farming reforms he made on his Holkham estate.

Aged 22, having inherited 30,000 Norfolk acres from his father (who had expired following a most uncomfortable bout of 'constipation which medicine could not remove'), Coke set about transforming the property.

Coke believed that it was the landowner's duty to improve the lives of those living on his estate. The landlord provided fields and buildings while the tenant provided seed, implements and labour. Coke wanted to set an example as a progressive landowner with principles based on stewardship and local pride. He shared and promoted new ideas. He gave his tenant farmers leases of up to forty years on the basis that if they knew they were there for a long time they would be more inclined to invest properly in the land. He also organised events to encourage new farming methods, such as a sheep-shearing competition called Coke's Clippings. His tenant farms were models to other landlords and he spent huge amounts of money renovating Holkham's rundown property.

When Coke took over Holkham the land was in poor condition. It was said that there were two rabbits fighting for every blade of grass. There was no wheat and just a few miserable crops of rye. The only livestock were a few undernourished milking cows.

Coke purchased large quantities of manure, grew clover and trebled his livestock, giving rise to the Norfolk proverb: 'Muck is the mother of money.' Coke was one of the first people to use newfangled drilling machines to plant crops such as wheat and turnips. Drilling saved time and seed. It produced uniform crops and could increase yields tenfold. Towards the end of the eighteenth century a group of farmers living near Sheffield had been grinding up bone left over from cutlery handles and spreading

it on their fields. It made excellent fertiliser. Coke heaped bone meal on his land thereby greatly improving Holkham's thin, sandy soil.

Within ten years Coke was growing fine crops of wheat. He moved on to livestock. Dressed in a common smock, he worked alongside his shepherds and cowhands, building a formidable flock of New Leicesters crossed with pure Norfolks, and a herd of Devons and Southdowns.

Coke was the first farmer to realise the advantages of mixing grasses such as cocksfoot and lucerne in order to produce the richest hay. He gave simple botanical lessons to his tenants' children, who scoured the countryside for seed.

Coke's tenants became the richest in England. He remarked: 'It has been objected against me that my tenants live too much like gentlemen, driving their own curricles and drinking port every day. I am proud to have such tenantry, and heartily wish that instead of drinking port they could afford to drink claret and champagne.' Coke could certainly afford champagne: Holkham's annual rental rose from £2,200 in 1776 to £20,000 in 1816.

Coke of Norfolk, as he became known, combined agriculture with a parliamentary career: he was MP for Norfolk for fifty years. He spoke mostly on local matters, and campaigned for civil liberties. He fought to relax England's excessively tough game laws with their severe penalties for poaching. Described as the 'greatest commoner in England' he was made the Earl of Leicester in 1837. He died five years later aged 88. His last words were: 'Well, perhaps I have talked too much.'

• Thomas Coke loved field sports and appears to have done little other than shoot while at Eton – he narrowly escaped expulsion after poaching a pheasant in Windsor Park. Upon leaving school he undertook a European grand tour financed by a great-aunt who bribed him with the enormous sum of £500 not to go to that slurry pit of immorality known as university.

• Coke could not be blamed for turning in his grave if he saw what had become of British farming in the twenty-first century. In 2011, rather than produce crops, around 67 per cent of farmed land – 15.3 million acres – was under a subsidised environmental incentive scheme of one kind or another. The European Union currently has no fewer than 56,000 such schemes in operation worth £409 million to landowners. Biodiversity has increased as a result, but this has led to today's big agricultural argument: what is more important – making the country look nice and safe with endless, restrictive environmental schemes, or providing enough food so that we don't starve? British farmers claim that UK agriculture is doomed unless we abandon limits on fertiliser usage, scrap the ban on genetically modified crops and start becoming a proper food-producing nation again.

WHUTTLED HIS CRAIG

THE LAST WOLF KILLED in Britain was dispatched by a hunter called MacQueen on the banks of the River Findhorn in the Scottish Highlands in 1743. The wolf, a huge black beast, was Public Enemy No. 1 having just killed two children.

MacQueen was a legendary hunter. He spoke of the kill: 'As I came through the slochk [ravine] I foregathered wi' the beast. My long dog there turned him. I buckled wi' him, and dirkit him, and syne whuttled his craig [cut his throat], and brought awa' his countenance [cut off his head] for fear he might come alive again, for they are very precarious creatures.'

Thanks to dramatic changes in land management, wolves were doomed in eighteenth-century Scotland. Their natural habitat, the huge Highland forests, were being cut down to produce charcoal for the iron-smelting industry.

• Legend has it that the last wolf killed in England was dispatched some time during the sixteenth century at Perry Oaks, latterly a sewage works and close to the site of Terminal 5, Heathrow Airport.

• There has been talk in recent years of reintroducing wolves into the wild in the Scottish Highlands as a tourist attraction. The idea has not gone down well with sheep farmers.

• The best place for wolf hunting in England was the wolds of east Yorkshire which were said to be infested with the beasts during the Middle Ages.

• The last brown bear to be hunted in England was killed around 1050.

ESSENTIAL MAD DOG INFO

'To know whether a Dog is mad or not – Dogs suspected of being mad are frequently killed, leaving persons bitten in a dreadful uncertainty, whether the dogs were or were not really mad. The following experiment has been supposed conclusive: rub the mouth, teeth, and gums of the dead dog with a little roast or boiled meat, and offer this meat, so rubbed, to another dog, who will eat it without reluctance if the dead dog was not mad, but will refuse it, and run away howling, if the dead dog was really mad.'

From the New Family Receipt Book, *1810*

FISHING FIVE

The five stages of the trout fisherman's casting career, according to John Stirling, author of 1929 angling classic *Fifty Years With The Rod*:

1. The novice angler should be able to cast a worm deftly, and without injury to the bait, on a spot six inches across and at a distance of about six yards from the angler's feet.
2. With a little more experience, and in a slight wind, he should cast a fly delicately to a similar spot ten yards away.
3. Then he should manage twenty yards, without a following breeze, so that the fly will alight as softly as a natural insect.
4. The penultimate stage is to do the same with a cross wind and with troublesome vegetation surrounding him.
5. Finally, he should be able to carry out these operations with either hand uppermost when using a two-hand rod, or to be able to fish with equal proficiency with a single-hand rod from either end of a boat.

Stirling was the much-revered president of the Scottish Anglers' Association during the years following the First World War.

COUNTRY SPORT

'Hunting for spectacles is the only sport left for old age.'

Lord Grey of Fallodon (1862–1933), longest-ever serving Foreign Secretary (1905–16) and noted countryman, fisherman and ornithologist, whose most famous photograph shows him with a robin perched on his twitcher's hat

EXCELLENT MARRIAGES

The largest ever landed estate in Britain was that under the control of George Granville William Sutherland Leveson-Gower, third Duke of Sutherland, in the latter half of the nineteenth century. Sutherland's Scottish landholdings in 1878 were 1,176,454 acres in Sutherland and 149,000 acres in Ross, while south of the border he owned 17,495 acres in Shropshire, 12,744 in Staffordshire, 1,853 in Yorkshire, and just one acre in Buckinghamshire. These properties were the result of four generations of excellent marriages by the Gowers, said to have been the fastest upwardly mobile family in Britain.

• The nineteenth century saw huge estates in the hands of women such as Baroness Willoughby de Eresby, who owned 132,000 acres of Lincolnshire. About 10 per cent of rural Britain was owned by females in 1872.

• Today's largest landowners are public bodies, but they own peanuts when compared to Sutherland:

1. Forestry Commission: 2,400,000 acres; 60 per cent in Scotland, 26 per cent in England and the remainder in Wales.
2. Ministry of Defence: 592,800 acres in the UK (and another 250,000 leased acres in Canada). During the period of the British Empire the government needed only 165,000 acres of Britain to train its entire military force. One wonders what the MOD does with more than half a million acres. Time to sell?
3. National Trust: 630,000 acres.
4. Crown Estate: 265,000 acres with nearly 800 tenant farms.
5. The Duke of Buccleuch: 240,000 acres in England and Scotland (Europe's largest private landowner).

These are followed by The Duke of Atholl (145,700 acres) and Prince Charles's Duchy of Cornwall, which lags behind with 133,602 mostly West Country acres.

• Of all the land in Britain, 70 per cent is owned by 1 per cent of the population.

• As of 2011, British farmland was worth £5,000–7,000 per acre, an increase of more than 100 per cent in a decade. Prime arable land in the South West can go for up to £11,000 per acre and rising. 'Farmers are still the primary occupiers of farmland', says Crispin Holborow, head of UK estate agents Savills. 'However, farms in parts of the UK, such as the West Country, are now often bought by what we term the amenity or hobby farmer, who is looking to live in a well-positioned house with up to a few hundred acres. For buyers of English estates today, it's about owning the trophy asset, which must work as a home, but also at least hold its value.'

• The total land area of Britain amounts to 59,557 million acres:
England – 32,056 million acres
Scotland – 19,070 million acres
Wales – 5,099 million acres
Northern Ireland – 3,332 million acres

• The richest, though by no means the largest landowner in Britain, is the Duke of Westminster, who regularly features in the top ten of the *Sunday Times* Rich List with a pot of around £7 billion. Much of this wealth is made up of ninety acres in central London.

• The British population – circa 60 million – is housed in 24 million dwellings, which sit on 4.4 million acres, meaning that less than 8 per cent of UK land has been developed.

• Gardens take up more than one million acres of the UK.

FRAIL SNOWDROPS

When haughty expectations prostrate lie,
And grandeur crouches like a guilty thing,
Oft shall the lowly weak, till nature bring
Mature release, in fair society
Survive, and Fortune's utmost anger try;
Like these frail snowdrops that together cling,
And nod their helmets, smitten by the wing
Of many a furious whirl-blast sweeping by.

From 'On Seeing A Tuft Of Snowdrops In A Storm', by William Wordsworth, 1819

• The snowdrop is a symbol of hope. Legend has it that when Eve was about to give up hope that cold winters in the Garden of Eden would never end, an angel appeared and transformed the snowflakes into snowdrops, proving that winter will eventually turn into spring. The 'drop' in snowdrop comes from 'eardrop', the old word for earring. Regarded these days as a wild flower, snowdrops were originally garden escapees. They were not recorded as growing wild in Britain until the 1770s. In the Catholic Church the flower is a symbol of Candlemas, 2nd February. As a result of this, anti-Catholics have brutally dubbed the entirely innocent snowdrop as a death token, or 'a corpse in its shroud'. It is because of this that some Protestants believe it is unlucky to bring snowdrops into the house.

• 'When Candlemas is come and gone, the snow lieth on a hot stone', i.e. snow after 2nd February is unlikely to stay long.

NOT OVER RICH

'The Country Farmer's Son' is a sixteenth-century folksong
that promotes the virtues of the simple life:

> I would not be a monarch great
> With crown upon my head,
> And earls to wait upon my state,
> In broidered robes of red.
> For he must bear full many a care,
> His toil is never done;
> 'Tis better I trow behind the plough
> A Country Farmer's son.
>
> I would not be a merchant rich,
> And eat off silver plate,
> And ever dread, when laid abed,
> Some freakish turn of fate:
> One day on high, then ruin nigh,
> Now wealthy, now undone;
> 'Tis better for me at ease to be
> A Country Farmer's Son.
>
> I trudge about the farm all day
> To know that all things thrive;
> A maid I see that pleaseth me,
> Why then I'm fain to wive.
> Not over rich, I do not itch
> For wealth, but what is won
> By honest toil from out of the soil,
> A Country Farmer's Son.

A SINGULAR CHARM AMONG TOOLS

'Scythes have a charm quite singular among tools. Their shape alone might account for it; smooth and sinuous, with deadly possibilities lurking somewhere in their aspect, they do certainly fascinate. It is a severe and simple beauty theirs, as good as that of Greek statues ... Perhaps in all the world there is no other thing so intimately associated with the summer at its best. At sight of this tool one does not always think consciously of the deep meadows and the June days, but it is odd if some of their beauty does not find its way into one's spirit. And from the brave English weather that they recall, a feeling of kinship with the generations of men who have rejoiced in it with scythes in their hands is never very far remote.'

From Change In The Village, *by George Bourne, 1912: described as a proto-socialist, Bourne, real name George Sturt (1863–1927), was one of the foremost commentators on rural Edwardian England.*

Scything tips:

- Keep the blade SHARP. Lay the blade on a bench or equivalent, and draw a proper scythe sharpening stone along the edge of the blade. It is worth sharpening frequently – every five minutes in the field – and the instrument will cut much more quickly. A sharp blade is the key to successful scything. You will cut through grass with amazing ease. As well as clearing weeds and harvesting hay quicker than with a strimmer, consider it as aerobic exercise. Mowing with a dull blade is hard work. Violently hacking down vegetation is invigorating at first but soon becomes exhausting.

- Adjust the blade properly for your height. There are three mounting points for the blade at the end of the snath (pole). Adjust the handles – the lower is supposed to be about the length of the blade from the end of the snath and the upper handle about the length of your forearm above that.

- Develop a smooth, effortless action. As your right leg goes forward a step, the scythe comes backwards; your left leg follows the scythe's cutting stroke. Swing from your torso, not from your arms.

- NEVER leave a scythe lying on the ground. Hang it up out of harm's way.

SOUTH IS BEST

IF YOU WANT A LONG, HEALTHY LIFE, move to rural South Cambridgeshire. According to a survey, South Cambridgeshire, where people live to an average of 82 years old, has the best quality of life in Britain based on good health, life expectancy, high employment, good school qualifications, and beneficial climate.

The top local authority areas for quality of life in 2011:

1. South Cambridgeshire
2. East Hertfordshire
3. Uttlesford, Essex
4. Aylesbury Vale, Buckinghamshire
5. Waverley, Surrey
6. Tandridge, Surrey
7. Mid Sussex
8. Chiltern, Buckinghamshire
9. East Cambridgeshire
10. Tonbridge and Malling, Kent

Halifax Building Society survey

One cannot fail to notice that these halcyon areas are in the southern half of England. Rural areas in the north tend to achieve high school exam ratings along with low population density and traffic flow, whereas rural southern areas perform better in the categories of earnings, employment, health and weather.

• Britain's largest rural homes can be found in the Chiltern local authority area in Buckinghamshire.

UNREAL

WANNABE FARMERS unable to afford up to £10,000 per acre for land can instead try 'virtual' farming with Farmville, an internet social network game. Members plough virtual land, harvest virtual crops and raise virtual livestock which produce virtual dung. Virtual subsidies are available for 'farmers' having a tough time. Around three million sad people worldwide spend their leisure time playing Farmville. Perhaps they would be better off with a long walk in the countryside.

ANTICIPATION RATHER THAN RAGE

The Spectator magazine's agony aunt Mary Killen offers advice to a wife whose landowner husband has become enraged by the sight of ramblers walking across his land, close to their house, on a long-forgotten footpath that has just been reopened by the local council:

'Most walkers are harmless types who stick to footpaths religiously. However, to distract your husband from the immediate annoyance of the new breed of militant rambler, why not suggest that he excavate, quite legally, several "mantraps" in the field in question but at some distance from the path. These should be four or five feet deep and will soon fill up with water, after which they may be covered with a camouflage of sticks and vegetation similar to those used in the book *Rogue Male* by Geoffrey Household. Your husband can then redirect his energies as the sight of approaching ramblers will begin to fill him with anticipation rather than rage.'

Reprinted by permission of HarperCollins Publishers Ltd © 1993, Mary Killen,
The Spectator Book of Solutions

A BEAUTIFUL VIEW

'The beauty of the British countryside is almost entirely due to the fact that it has been owned by families across generations – whether in the form of landed estates or family farms. Those who inherit property and pass it on have a motive to look after it that is quite different from the motive of the temporary resident. Ill-considered taxes have penalised inheritance, broken up the landed estates, and now threaten the family farm. A coherent Conservative policy must first try to reverse this process, so as to facilitate the long-term interest in the land across generations. Currently the National Trust and the Forestry Commission – both beneficiaries of inheritance tax – are the largest absentee landlords in the country.'

Philosopher Professor Roger Scruton, Countryside For All, The
Future Of Rural Britain, *published by Vintage, 2001*

USEFUL AND HEALTHFUL EXERCISE

FROM THE BEGINNING the lawnmower was designed to be a form of entertainment. Edwin Budding, inventor of the rotary mowing machine in 1830, wrote in his advertising blurb: 'Country gentlemen will find in using my machine an amusing useful and healthful exercise.'

Healthful? Budding's contraption was so heavy that it buggered the backs of a generation of country gentlemen. The landed classes breathed a sigh of relief when Scotsman Alexander Shanks invented the horse-drawn mower in 1842.

Budding, illegitimate son of a yeoman farmer, was a Gloucestershire textile foreman who based his mower on a machine that used blades to shear the nap from woollen cloth after weaving. Budding realised that the blades would have a similar effect on grass if mounted in a wheeled frame.

His first mower was nineteen inches wide and pushed from behind. Grass clippings were hurled forward into a box. Pushing it was extremely hard work, so Budding designed an extra handle in front of the machine so that a second person could help by pulling.

Having patented his machine, Budding granted the manufacturing rights to a Suffolk agricultural engineering firm called Ransomes, which was making ploughshares. Ransomes is now the world's largest lawn-care equipment manufacturer. Sadly, Budding did not live long enough to see his invention in mass production: he died in 1846 aged 50.

Several inventors, including Shanks, followed up with their own mowers. By the 1850s Budding's patents had lapsed. Thomas Green and Son of Leeds in 1859 produced their chain-driven Silens Messor, meaning 'silent cutter'. By the 1870s most gardens in Britain boasted a lawnmower – the 1874 *Beeton's Dictionary of Gardening* described the lawnmower as 'too well-known to need description'.

• The first petrol mower was produced by Ransomes in 1902. The gang mower, favourite of cricket clubs and public schools, was patented in 1914 by an American company called Worthington. Lawnmower sales soared after the First World War as people moved to the suburbs: everyone wanted a lawn. In 1921 Charles H. Pugh Ltd launched the Atco, a twenty-two-inch beauty costing a whopping £75. Within five years annual production had grown to tens of thousands. The rotary machine was invented in America in the 1940s whilst twenty years later saw the birth of sixties icon the Flymo.

• Before lawnmowers, keeping up a lawn was hideously expensive. In the eighteenth century, Blenheim Palace employed more than fifty labourers with scythes to cut the grass. At the height of summer the Blenheim lawns were

sheared every ten days by scythesmen using long, serrated blades. They worked in lines using a sawing motion, and had to stop regularly to sharpen the blades. The clippings were collected by the men's wives and children.

• Around 6,500 lawnmower accidents are reported each year in Britain, making it the most dangerous garden item. (The flowerpot comes second with 5,300 accidents.)

• The late poet Philip Larkin wrote a poem called 'The Mower', in which he describes killing a hedgehog with his Qualcast Commodore. Following this disaster he replaced the Qualcast with a

New Zealand machine called a Norlett. Larkin enjoyed lawn-mowing and had no time for ecosystems. He wrote to a friend in 1981: 'Must get the flamethrower serviced, and invest in a few gallon drums of Weedol.' Larkin's rusty, grass-encrusted Victa Powerplus is preserved in Hull University library archive.

• The rock band Genesis is the only group to have acknowledged the lawnmower. Their 1973 single 'I Know What I Like (In Your Wardrobe)' included the memorable line: 'Me, I'm just a lawnmower – you can tell me by the way I walk.' The lyrics by singer Peter Gabriel were in memory of a Genesis roadie called Jacob who could never hold down jobs. One of Jacob's previous occupations had been as a landscape gardener, in which he spent much of the time mowing lawns. He died from a heroin overdose while working in a doughnut shop.

MAKING YOUR GRASS GROW

IN THE FIRST HALF OF THE NINETEENTH CENTURY, about the time Edwin Budding was perfecting his lawnmower, a German chemist called Justus Von Liebig was developing chemical fertiliser to make grass grow even more. Liebig (1803–1873) discovered that nitrogen was an essential plant nutrient, and produced an ammonia-based plant feed. Though a commercial failure, his invention recognised the possibility of substituting chemical fertilisers for natural ones. His theories were to revolutionise agriculture.

• 2005 saw the death, aged 89, of Horace Hagedorn, the man who gave the gardening world Miracle-Gro, a product that dominated the home fertiliser market for decades. Hagedorn's liquid changed gardening, although critics claimed it damaged the soil. Hagedorn claimed that using his product would make vegetables and flowers grow 'bigger, better, faster'. Hagedorn eventually sold out for millions.

WONDER WALLS

DRYSTONE WALL BUILDING is one of the oldest construction methods known to mankind. An expert stone-waller can build about ten feet in a day, which entails lifting about three tons of stone. Here are some tips:

1. Measure out the base dimensions (width and length) of your wall. Mark the corners with wooden stakes. Run string between the stakes, or you can use limestone dust, to mark the edges of the wall. Use the string or limestone as markers to dig the base trench.

2. Dig a base trench four inches deep for walls eighteen inches high or lower, or eight inches deep for walls between eighteen inches and two-and-a-half feet high. Remove stones and roots from the trench and smooth the sides and bottom.

3. Fill the bottom of the four-inch deep trench with two inches of aggregate, or the bottom of the eight-inch deep trench with four inches of aggregate. Tamp the aggregate down. This provides drainage and stability for the wall.

4. Choose cornerstones the same width as your wall. Place them, on either end of the wall, on the aggregate with the flattest side down.

5. Starting on one end, lay base stones in two parallel rows. Keep a small gap between the rows. The base stones should fit tightly against one another. Lay a tie stone (a stone the same width as the trench) every yard for added stability and strength. The base stones don't have to be the same height; just arrange them so that they slope in towards the centre of the wall (the gap).

6. Fill the gap between the base stones with aggregate. The aggregate should be slightly deeper than the height of the base stones.

7. Use mixed grade stones to form the wall. You will alternate working on either end, laying one course at a time, meeting in the middle. Use stones horizontally and vertically, working across the width first, then increasing the length. Try to set stones side by side that naturally fit or join together.

8. Every yard or so, lay a tie stone. Do not stack stones directly on top of each other; stagger the stacking so only three stones form a joint. Continue slanting the stones towards the interior of the wall. Use aggregate stones to fill in gaps.

9. As you finish one course, check the level. The course does not have to be perfectly level, but you don't want big dips or waves.

10. Choose capstones with two flat surfaces, top and bottom. Fit them on the top to complete the wall. They should be the same width as the wall.

WAYNE GURNEY

Simple country folk will enjoy the World Gurning Championships held annually at the Egremont Crab Fair in the Lake District. Gurning – pulling faces – dates back to the thirteenth century. The championships are judged on nothing more than how hideous a person can make him or herself. The longest-running male UK champion is Cumbrian builder Tommy Mattinson, a surprisingly good-looking man, who has won the trophy eleven times, having broken the record set by his father Gordon. At the worst stage of his gurn Tommy is said to resemble Wayne Rooney sucking a lemon. A frightful sight indeed.

- Gurning is tough work. Such was her effort at pulling faces, sexagenarian grandmother Anne Woods, female winner of the 2010 Egremont Gurning Championships, collapsed afterwards with exhaustion.

- Traditional gurns include styles such as the 'Popeye' (puffed-out cheeks and crossed eyes), the 'American Werewolf' (nose contorted into a snout) and the 'duck face' (outwardly splayed lips and raised eyebrows, popular in Australia).

- The best gurners have no teeth, thus providing greater room for the jaw to move upwards. Some toothless gurners can cover their entire nose with their jaw. The 1990s UK champion Peter Jackman had his teeth removed to make his features easier to manoeuvre.

- Gurning is believed to have started in rural England as a result of people pulling faces while eating sour crabapples.

TERRIBLE

A 2010 survey revealed that 80 per cent of Britain's half a million ponds, both man-made and natural, were in a terrible condition and riddled with pollution. The report by the Centre for Ecology and Hydrology and Pond Conservation revealed that ponds were in poorest condition in intensive agricultural areas and where they were fed by water run-off from towns and roads.

- Globally, there are about 300 million standing water bodies, of which 90 per cent are ponds of less than ten hectares in area. Despite their small size, ponds represent 30 per cent of the global surface area of standing water.

SHAM DAIRYMAIDS

Belgravia magazine of 1867 offers us a view of the picnic:

'The picnic … is unquestionably Great British in its origin. It is a hardy national institution, and no puny derivative from the French *fête champêtre* as some Gallomaniacs have affected to believe. To the French is due, no doubt, that sickly piece of practical sentimentality known to our grandmothers as a syllabub, a ceremony now as extinct as the dodo. How wearisome it must have been, that parody of Arcadia enacted on the lawn of an English country house, where London fine ladies, turned into Phyllis and Chloë for the nonce, exhibited their be-ribboned crooks for the admiration of Bond Street Corydons; where sham dairymaids, dressed by a court milliner, played the pretty rustic with a mock simplicity, and where the only touch of nature was shown by the flower-decked cow—poor thing!—when she avenged her gilt horns and garlanded neck by kicking over the milk pail and by charging the musicians!'

The syllabub ceremony was popular in England in the sixteenth and seventeenth centuries. Sugar and wine were mixed in a large bowl. This was placed under a cow and filled with fresh milk. The disgusting concoction was consumed while still warm.

• If you prefer lashings of ginger beer on your picnic, follow these instructions for making your own:

> Put two ounces of baker's yeast into a jar and add two cupfuls of water, two teaspoons of sugar and two teaspoons of powdered ginger. Feed the plant (this refers, essentially, to the yeast) daily for a week with a teaspoonful each of ginger and sugar. After a week, strain the liquid through muslin, keeping the residue to start two new plants. Add to the liquid the juice of two lemons, two pints of boiling water and a pound of sugar, and a gallon of cold water. Leave for three hours before bottling. Drink after six days. [Caution: ginger beer is highly explosive if allowed to get too warm. The author remembers an incident during his college days when a ginger beer plant went off with such a bang that shards of glass ended up embedded in the walls.]

WOVEN FROM BRAMBLES

'FOR COUNTRY WEAR, the tweed suit is essential. Once tweed was woven from brambles onto barbed wire, and its spines were capable of penetrating the thickest underwear. Physical agony forced many into wearing pinstripe suits in the country, leading to derision. Now, happily, synthetic fibres are used to weave tweeds which are not only kind to delicate skin but display a sheen somewhat like that of a starling's breast, and are guaranteed to attract attention.'

Harry Chance, The Bounder's Companion, *Hutchinson, 1983*

ELECTRIC HARE

'The fur of the hare is more strongly electrical than the hair of any other animal. If you apply the point of a finger to his side in frosty weather, the hairs are immediately strongly attracted towards it from all points, and closely embrace the finger on every side.'

Correspondence in The Gentleman's Magazine, *1788*

• Hare trivia: the Waterloo Cup, the greatest annual event in the coursing calendar (until the bunny-huggers banned the sport, along with placing major restrictions on hunting in 2005) was named after Liverpool's Waterloo Hotel whose proprietor, William Lynn, launched the event in 1836. Encouraged by the extra trade generated by the Waterloo Cup, Lynn turned to racing. The following year he organised the first Grand Liverpool Steeplechase, a terrifying race with huge jumps which was to become the Grand National. During the nineteenth century, hare coursing was one of the most popular working-class sports in Britain, with more than 150 clubs attracting up to 80,000 people.

COMIC REMAINS

QUOTE FROM COMEDIAN RUSSELL HOWARD on a show he gave at Shropshire's Harper Adams Agricultural College: 'The audience was stupid, right-wing and full of cider. I thought it would be a bit of a laugh to poke fun at the merits of fox-hunting. To which they said they were going to kill me, sexually abuse me and show my remains to other comics who dared to mock their country ways. I feared for my life so I cried "Hey, Freddie Flintoff's a good guy" and it was all fine again.'

• While Cirencester Agricultural College is tame by comparison, it is generally accepted that Harper Adams, outside the Shropshire town of Newport, boasts some of Britain's worst-behaved farm students. Vodka-fuelled all-night parties accompanied by the sound of revving short wheelbase Land Rovers are common in Newport. Pity the poor residents whose neighbours let their houses for student accommodation.

UNWANTED IMMIGRANTS

Miscellaneous foreign animals occasionally found in Britain
having escaped from farms and zoos:

Raccoon dogs: native to Asia and Russia.
Spotted in Oxfordshire and West Berkshire.

Siberian chipmunks: can carry rabies and other nasty diseases.
Seen in Berkshire, Wiltshire and Cheshire.

South American coypus: there have been numerous sightings
in the past twenty years, mainly in East Anglia.
They were originally brought to the UK by fur
farmers in the 1930s.

CANAL TRIVIA

BRITAIN'S INLAND WATERWAYS include around 2,200 miles of canals and rivers with 1,654 locks, 54 tunnels, 3,115 bridges and 417 aqueducts.

Canal towpaths are used by 13 million people every year for walking the dog or watching the boats: 60 per cent of waterway visitors say they exercise more regularly because they live near a canal.

Half the population of the UK lives within five miles of a canal or river.

Approximately 35,000 boats and 30,000 canoes regularly use the UK's canals, which are actually busier now than they were at the height of the Industrial Revolution. Canals are being restored more rapidly these days than they were being built two centuries ago.

In 2010 British Waterways spent millions removing 30,000 tons of fly-tipping (equivalent to the weight of 4,000 Routemaster buses) from canals and rivers.

Almost two million tons of freight is carried on UK waterways each year, a tiny amount when compared to the 30 million tons being moved annually in the early nineteenth century.

British Waterways is the third-largest owner of listed buildings in the UK after the National Trust and the Church of England.

HOMELY PLEASURES

CHARLES KINGSLEY (1819–1875), author of *The Water-Babies*, village parson and a great countryman, declared: 'I have many loves and fly-fishing is one of them. It brings peace and harmony to my being, which I can then pass on to others.' Kingsley spent much of his life as rector of Eversley in Hampshire. In a classic essay titled 'Chalk Stream Studies' he argued that it was more pleasurable to fish on a Home Counties river such as the Test rather than in the grander waters of Scotland:

'Let the Londoner have his six weeks every year among crag and heather, and return with lungs expanded and muscles braced to his nine months' prison. The countryman, who needs no such change of air and scene, will prefer more homely pleasures. Dearer to him than wild cataracts or Alpine glens are the still hidden streams which Bewick has immortalised in his vignettes, and Creswick in his pictures. The long grassy shallow, paved with yellow gravel, where he wades up between low walls of fern-fringed rock, beneath nut and oak and alder, to the low bar over which the stream comes swirling and dimpling, as the water-ouzel flits piping before him, and the murmur of the ringdove comes soft and sleepy through the wood – there, as he wades, he sees a hundred sights and hears a hundred tones which are hidden from the traveller on the dusty highway above. The traveller fancies that he has seen the country. So he has; the outside of it, at least: but the angler only sees the inside. The angler only is brought close face to face with the flower, and bird, and insect life of the rich river banks, the only part of the landscape where the hand of man has never interfered, and the only part in general which never feels the drought of summer.'

YEW EAT, YOU DIE

YEW is the most curious of the plants poisonous to animals. The berries are deadly to cattle, though harmless to pigs. Likewise sheep, turkeys, deer, moose and elk can eat yew while horses have been known to die merely from gnawing on the bark of a yew tree. Yew is also poisonous to dogs, though it is unlikely that your pet will eat any (unless it's a Labrador, in which case it will eat anything).

Yew contains toxic alkaloids, which mainly affect the heart. Consumption of as little as 1–10g/kg of bodyweight for cattle and 0.5–2g/kg for horses is lethal. Symptoms of yew poisoning include muscle trembling, incoordination, nervousness, breathing difficulty, slow heart rate, vomiting, diarrhoea and convulsions. Note: yew is also poisonous to humans.

- The toxins in yew can be put to good use – yew trimmings are used to make the active ingredient taxotere for the anti-cancer drug Tamoxifen, the world's largest-selling breast cancer medication.

- Yews have always been popular for landscaping because they can withstand trimming and are easily transplanted. They can tolerate virtually all urban pollution except road salt.

- Longbows were traditionally made from yew. Bow-makers suffered poisoning from frequent handling of the wood.

- 'I always think of yew as the "little black dress" of the garden.' *Gardening writer James Bartholomew*

CLAPPED OUTDOORS

UNTIL THE END OF THE NINETEENTH CENTURY the children of the rural poor would be armed with clapperboards and used as scarecrows. In return for pennies they would spend March to May bird-scaring, then again in November over newly sown wheat. Victorian poet Edward Capern describes their work in his poem 'The Little Scarecrow Girl':

> She's up in yonder field,
> 'Mid the new-sown corn,
> She'll be there until the eve,
> She has been there since morn.
> O the pretty little creature with the bright blue eye,
> I heard her noisy clapper and her scarecrow cry.
> I paused to mark the child—
> She was very pale and young;
> She told me she was 'six'
> With her merry little tongue.
> In her hand she held her hat,
> Which the wild wind sway'd;
> And purple were the feet
> Of the scarecrow maid.
> More happy than a queen,
> Though scanty was her food,
> The child that sang her song
> To that clapper music rude.
> This, the maiden's simple lay,
> As she warbled in her nook,
> 'Here, clapping every day,
> I scare the robber rook.'

Edward Capern (1819–1894) was a former post office worker who became famous as the 'Postman Poet'. His most reproduced work was a patriotic epic titled 'The Lion Flag Of England', 1855, which was published as a broadsheet and sent to the troops in the Crimea. The poem so moved Prime Minister Lord Palmerston that he awarded Capern a pension of £60 per year from the Civil List.

• Edwardian countryside writer Frances A. Bardswell once asked a farmer what kind of scarecrows worked best. 'He told me that there is nothing to beat large pieces of white paper spread over the ground, and held down with stones. "The birds," he said, "do not so soon get used to this as to most other things, such as bits of glass and metal crowded together to make jingly noises."'

• Obituary of a vicar, the Rev. Favell Hopkins in the *Hull Packet*, 9th June, 1812: 'For many years such had been Mr Hopkins' propensity to parsimony that, although possessed of considerable funded property, he grudged himself the common necessaries of life; and often while walking the streets exhibited more the appearance of a miserable mendicant than a respectable clergyman. Walking one Sunday morning to do duty at a parish church in Cambridgeshire, he saw in a field a scarecrow; going up to the figure he took off its hat, examined it, then looked at his own, and finding the advantage to be in favour of the former, he fairly exchanged the one for the other.'

• Cheshire man Christopher Strong fell foul of the law in 2007 after dressing up his scarecrow as a traffic cop. Mr Strong, 58, clad the one-legged straw dummy in a fluorescent yellow jacket from Halfords and a novelty plastic police hat. He added a striped tie, epaulettes, a homemade badge reading 'Scarecrow Traffic Policy', a speed gun fashioned from a lady's hairdryer, and a broken solar light from his garden. Brimming with enthusiasm, he stuck it on top of his hedge to see if it would deter speeding motorists.

Plod failed to see the joke. After ordering Mr Strong to remove his creature, officers warned that 'he' could be accused of trying to impersonate a policeman. 'The officers were rather brusque and said they had received several complaints from motorists. They told me to remove the hat and hairdryer or I may be accused of impersonating a police officer. I explained that it was a scarecrow with a head full of straw and one leg, but they were not in the least amused.'

Police insisted later that there had been a misunderstanding: 'We did not intend Mr Strong to think that his scarecrow would be prosecuted', a spokesman said.

DIG AT DEFRA?

'Farming looks mighty easy when your plough is a pencil and you're a thousand miles from the corn field.'

General Dwight D. Eisenhower, 34th US President

CHEESE ROLL

The strangest sport enjoyed by English country folk was the Cooper's Hill Cheese Rolling contest that was held annually on the Spring Bank Holiday weekend. It was meant as a bit of fun for the local village of Brockworth but, like all things in the global society, it got out of hand and competitors started flying in from all over the world. Then the punters complained about the newly-introduced £20 entry fee.

In 2010 the event was cancelled because of health 'n' safety concerns. The organising committee received death threats. 'Since we announced an entry fee, we have been bombarded with hostility', a spokesman complained. 'The event got too big, the management got beyond us and for every offer of help there were two demands for extra stuff to be done.'

Cheese rolling is the perfect sport for canon fodder peasantry with a low IQ and a high pain threshold. A round of Double Gloucester cheese was rolled off the top of Cooper's Hill and competitors raced down after it. The first person over the finishing line won the cheese. Competitors were supposed to catch the cheese, but nobody ever did, since a Double Gloucester at full pelt can reach 70mph.

Most competitors (and quite a few spectators) suffered injuries including sprained ankles, broken bones and concussion. An observer described the event as: 'Twenty young men chasing a cheese off a cliff and tumbling two hundred yards to the bottom, where they are scraped up by paramedics and packed off to hospital.'

• To demonstrate that cheese-rolling needs to return to its roots and does not require an 'organising committee', a clandestine contest took place at Cooper's Hill over Spring Bank Holiday 2011. Contestants said it was the best cheese roll in years. Amazingly, there were no injuries.

• During the Second World War rationing prevented the use of real cheese at Cooper's Hill. Instead, they used a wooden 'cheese' with a token slice of Double Gloucester in the middle.

• An infinitely more challenging rural contest is the annual Wrekin Barrel Race which takes place near the author's home in Shropshire every year. The race celebrates a 200-year tradition when beer kegs would have been hauled to the top of the Wrekin for the annual piss-ups known as the Wrekin Wakes. These days a team of four have to haul a nine-gallon firkin of ale weighing 50 kilograms from the base to the summit at 1,235 feet above sea level. The route is steep and can take up to half an hour. The race day includes a category known as The Lunatic, which is open to individuals. Only a hardy few take up this challenge to carry a full barrel single-handed to the top. Health and safety dictates that each person has to be accompanied by a second equipped with a first aid kit.

VICTORIAN COCK-UP

19TH APRIL IS PRIMROSE DAY, established in memory of Prime Minister Benjamin Disraeli who died on this Spring day in 1881. People paid tribute to Disraeli by wearing a primrose, supposedly his favourite flower. This turned out to be nonsense as Disraeli had no strong views on primroses. The misunderstanding arose after Queen Victoria sent a primrose wreath to Disraeli's funeral with a note stating they were 'his favourite flowers'. Evidently, the monarch was thinking not of her Prime Minister but of her late husband, Prince Albert, who was indeed partial to a primrose.

• The American poet Henry Cuyler Bunner (1855–1896) was moved to write:

'And all England, so they say, Yearly blooms on Primrose Day'.

A TYPICAL ENGLISH SUMMER?

Oft have I seen when fields of golden corn
Were fit to reap, and ready to be born,
The warring squadrons of the winds contend.
And from the roots the wealthy harvest rend;
Then boisterous tempests with a whirl-wind bear
Light straw and stubble through the cloudy air,
Oft from the sky descends a dreadful shower,
And mustered clouds from sea recruit their power
With hideous storms.

Virgil: eighteenth-century translation

TRAGEDY

THE 1940 POLICE shooting of a Hampshire tenant farmer over his refusal to allow his beloved meadow to be ploughed up to help the war effort was one of the greatest rural tragedies of the Second World War.

Bachelor George Walden, 65, had spent all his life on Borough Farm, Itchen Stoke, so he was distraught when the County War Agricultural Committee ordered him to plough up four acres of grassland to plant crops. When he refused, his landlord, a local grandee called Sir Anthony Tichborne, served him with a notice to quit.

Walden had a nervous breakdown. He barricaded himself into his house with his shotgun for company. A committee representative and two police constables went to the farm to evict him, and so began the incident known as the Itchen Stoke Shooting.

Seeing police in his yard, Walden fired his gun. A PC was taken to hospital with pellets in his leg. More officers arrived. They tried to smoke out Walden with tear gas. Walden put on his Government-issue gas mask and took another pot-shot, this time winging a police inspector. After a twelve-hour siege the police broke into the house. There was a brief exchange of gunfire in which two more officers were peppered. Walden was shot dead. The inquest jury returned a verdict of justifiable homicide. Indicating that Walden was entirely in the wrong, they sent their best wishes to the police constable who was recovering from his shotgun injuries.

• The Second World War County War Agricultural Committees – known as 'War Ags' – were unpopular with farmers, who viewed committee members as nincompoop bureaucrats with scant knowledge of farming. War Ags earned a reputation for forcing farmers to do stupid things such as ploughing up grassland in order to plant potatoes in four inches of soil. Crops frequently failed. From 1940, following the Defence of the Realm Act, around 13,000 farmers, covering a million acres of land, were thrown off their properties for failing to meet demanding production targets set by the Government during the 'Dig for Victory' campaign. In a supreme example of government nastiness, farmers were invited to 'grade' – i.e. grass up – their neighbours according to how efficiently they were producing food. Those graded 'C' were evicted.

• The most successful food organisations of the Second World War were the pig clubs, in which members could keep half the meat for themselves having handed over the rest to the Government. By 1943, 5,000 clubs – including one run by the Royal Household – were tending 120,000 pigs.

• For a taste of the Second World War you can try making Lord Woolton Pie, a carroty stew created in 1941 by the Savoy Hotel's chef and named after food minister Lord Woolton, former managing director of a North of England chain store. People thought Woolton's pie was a bit of a joke, but it was so substantial and gravyish that it convinced everyone they were eating meat.

Official recipe for Lord Woolton Pie, published in *The Times*, 6th April, 1941:

'Take 1lb each of diced potatoes, cauliflower, swedes and carrots; three or four spring onions; one teaspoonful of vegetable extract and one teaspoonful of oatmeal. Cook all together for ten minutes with just enough water to cover. Stir occasionally to prevent the mixture from sticking. Allow to cool; put into a pie dish, sprinkle with chopped parsley and cover with a crust of potatoes or wholemeal pastry. Bake in a moderate oven until the pastry is nicely brown and serve hot with brown gravy.'

SAFEST

The lowest burglary rates per 10,000 households are in Scotland's Western Isles (2.7) followed by North Wiltshire (6.2) and the Orkney Islands (6.5). The highest burglary rates are in Haringey, London (422 per 10,000 households).

SMOKED OUT

On the basis that anything enjoyable is almost bound to harm health, a French environmental survey reveals that eating barbecued food causes cancer. Outdoor types are warned that a two-hour blast of the barbie can release the same amount of dioxins as 220,000 cigarettes. The study was based on grilling four large steaks, four turkey breasts and eight large sausages. Researchers discovered that the average concentration of dioxins in the vicinity of the barbecue was up to seven times higher than the level authorised for public incinerators. But your chances of surviving are reasonably high. A researcher commented, 'If you have a barbecue once or twice a week through the summer, and all crowd round it and inhale the fumes, then over ten or twenty years maybe that would do something.'

• Danish toxicologists have declared that wood-burning stoves, essential heating in any twenty-first century country house, can cause heart disease and cancer. Until recently, little was known about the potentially harmful effects of breathing in wood smoke but scientist Professor Steffen Loft suggests tiny airborne specks in the smoke are small enough to be inhaled into the deepest parts of the lungs. He points out that in developing countries where wood fires are used for cooking, smoke is a major cause of disease.

You must use your stove correctly. By cutting up wood into small pieces, using only dry wood, and ensuring a good air supply to the combustion, dangerous particle emissions are reduced.

GREAT EXPEDITIONS

CHARLES DICKENS was a great walker. He routinely strode up to twenty miles a day, claiming that fresh air was essential to his writing. He sometimes left his London house at 2 a.m. to walk thirty miles to arrive at his country estate, Gad's Hill Place, near Rochester, Kent, in time for lunch. 'I have discovered that the seven miles between Maidstone and Rochester is one of the most beautiful walks in all England', he declared.

Dickens adored Kent. He wrote, 'Kent, Sir, everybody knows Kent: apples, cherries, hops and women.'

DOGGONE

B e warned that if you shoot a dog that is worrying your sheep you may be committing an offence and are likely to be charged with criminal damage. Your defence must show that you were protecting your livestock. You must also notify police within forty-eight hours of the shooting.

Note: a rifle conditioned only for the shooting of vermin would not be allowed to shoot a dog. Generally, if a dog is in a field with livestock and the owner is not in close control of the animal then it is reasonable to assume that the dog is 'out of control' and can be legally shot by the landowner.

> • Cats have less protection in British law than dogs. If you run one over you are not obliged to report the matter to the police as you are with a dog. But you are committing criminal damage if you shoot a domestic, collar-wearing puss for pestering your pheasants.

PIG PARADISE

Piggy Lore:

1. They say that pigs can 'see' the wind. When a storm is approaching pigs become restless.

2. The piglet that suckles from its mother's front teat will be the strongest in the litter.

3. Kill your pig when there is an R in the month if you want the best pork.

> • The narrator in the 1995 pig movie blockbuster *Babe* mentions pigs believing that the sooner they grow 'large and fat', the sooner they are taken into 'Pig Paradise, a place so wonderful that no pig has ever thought to come back'.

USELESS DISQUISITIONS

TROUT FISHERMEN agonising over whether to place a Greenwell's Glory, a Black Pennell, or a Silver Butcher on their line should heed the words of Victorian angling writer Thomas Tod Stoddart, who had no patience for people who fussed over such intricacies:

> 'There is no real service done to the angler, as regards trouting flies, by a multiplication of their names and varieties, or by useless disquisitions upon certain virtues peculiar to this or that imitation; I regard as unessential and elaborately trifling the attempts made by many theoretical writers on the subject of angling, to sort out and classify, according to the month, the different ephemeral and water insects which they think it necessary should be included in the stock of the fly-fisher. I am of opinion that, with a hare-lug, a brown and a black hackle, it being a matter of indifference whether the wing adapted to them is formed of the brown mallard, the woodcock, landrail, or grouse feather, or indeed whether the hackles are provided with wings at all.'

Stoddart (1810–1880), Edinburgh-born angler and poet, was an early campaigner against river pollution, particularly on his beloved Tweed which, by the end of his life, was clogging up with the Clyde's industrial filth.

• Coarse fishermen will tell you that the best way to catch carp is to bait your hook with cat food. Turkey-flavoured Kitekat works well, but tuna Whiskas is best. Dog biscuits are good for carp and chub. Barbel are supposed to find Spam and any other luncheon meat, sausages, meatballs, black pudding, etc. irresistible.

FROSTY FALLACY

W.D. (Bill) Campbell, a naturalist and schoolteacher from Charlbury, Oxfordshire, who, for thirty years from 1964, wrote *The Guardian*'s weekly column 'A Country Diary', disputed the theory that a hard winter kills bugs, thus helping crops to flourish. He claimed that quite the opposite could happen:

'I can think of some ways in which prolonged frosts favour the survival of underground insect pests such as leather-jackets, wireworms and the pupae of various moths. ... The frozen crust of the soil, even if only a few inches deep, ensures the safety of the pests below from probing beaks of rooks and starlings. But there now exists scientific evidence that freezing is not necessarily lethal either to minute invertebrate pests such as aphids, or the even tinier spores of fungal diseases. Samples of such aerial plankton (including non-pests such as tiny spiders) taken from a great height where the thin atmosphere is well below freezing, on being returned to ground-level in an apparently dead, frozen solid state, rapidly thaw and become actively alive. The best illustration of this ability of some animal life to survive being frozen solid occurred in the exceptionally prolonged spell of hard frost during the winter of 1962–3. On a bank in the corner of my garden lay a sheet of corrugated iron, and I lifted it in search of any items which might be of value to my hungry thrushes and robins. But what I found was a mass of hundreds of garden snails stuck together, and all in their sealed-up dormant condition. I took about half a dozen into school to show my class and fortunately did not stress the apparent beneficial effect of the weather. The arithmetic lesson then proceeded, but after about ten minutes the class appeared to lose application to their sums, and all eyes were directed to my desk – it was crawling with active snails.'

From A Country Diary, *published by Fourth Estate, copyright 1994 Guardian News & Media Ltd*

CHEAP WEED

IF YOU'RE SHORT OF CASH you can try eating chickweed, one of the most common garden weeds. In Victorian times chickweed was sold on London streets as a salad vegetable. Cooked properly, with plenty of butter, it can taste like spinach.

Chickweed pesto:
2 cloves of garlic, 3 tablespoons of pine nuts or sunflower seeds, ¼ tsp salt,
2 packed cups of chopped fresh chickweed, ½ cup olive oil and
½ cup Parmesan cheese. Mix in a blender and serve over pasta
or use it as a dip. Tastes refreshingly rustic.

• As a medical preparation chickweed (*stellaria media*) is good for the skin.

• Chickweed can help predict the weather. According to an 1810 publication called *The New Family Receipt Book*, the plant makes an excellent barometer: 'When the flower expands boldly and fully, no rain will happen for four hours; if it continues in that open state no rain will disturb the summer's day; when it half conceals its miniature flower, the day is generally showery; but when it entirely shuts up, or veils the white flowers with its green mantle it means heavy rain.'

HOW TO MAKE A FIRE

'FIRE-LIGHTING, however simple, is an operation requiring some skill; a fire is readily made by laying a few cinders at the bottom in open order; over this a few pieces of paper, and over that again eight or ten pieces of dry wood; over the wood, a course of moderate-sized pieces of coal, taking care to leave hollow spaces between for air at the centre; and taking care to lay the whole well back in the grate, so that the smoke may go up the chimney, and not into the room. This done, fire the paper with a match from below, and, if properly laid, it will soon burn up; the stream of flame from the wood and paper soon communicating to the coals and cinders, provided there is plenty of air at the centre.'

Mrs Beeton's Book of Household Management, *1861*

MARKET DAY IN VICTORIAN ENGLAND

This epic description of the Victorian countryside appeared in *The Rural Life of England*, 1838, by William Howitt, a Derbyshire farmer's son who became a prolific nineteenth-century writer and poet:

'There are few things which give one such a feeling of the prosperity of the country, as seeing the country people pour into a large town on market-day. There they come, streaming along all the roads that lead to it from the wide country round. The foot-paths are filled with a hardy and homely succession of pedestrians, men and women, with their baskets on their arms, containing their butter, eggs, apples, mushrooms, walnuts, nuts, elderberries, blackberries, bundles of herbs, young pigeons, fowls, or whatever happens to be in season. There

are boys and girls too, similarly loaded, and also with baskets of birds' nests in spring, cages of young birds, and old birds, baskets of tame rabbits, and bunches of cowslips, primroses, and all kinds of flowers, and country productions imaginable.

'The carriage-road is equally alive, with people riding and driving along; farmers and country gentlemen, country clergymen, parish overseers, and various other personages, drawn to the market-town by some real or imagined business, rattling forward on horseback, or in carriages of various kinds, gigs, and spring-carts, and carts without springs. There are carriers' wagons, and covered carts without end, many of them showing from their open fronts, whole troops of women snugly seated; while their dogs chained beneath, go struggling and barking along, pushing their heads forward in their collars every minute as if they would hang themselves. This is in the morning; and in the afternoon, you see them pouring out again, and directing their course to many a far-off hamlet. But there is a wide difference between coming in and going out. The wagons and carts go heavily and soberly, for they are laden with good solid commodities, groceries and draperies, mops, brushes, hardware and crockery, newspapers for the politicians, and sundry parcels of teas, sugars, and soaps, and such etceteras for the village shops; but the farmers go riding and driving out three times as fast as they came in, for they are primed with good dinners, and strong beer. They have chaffered, and smoked, and talked with the great grazier, and the great corn-factor, and their horses are full of corn too, and away they go, in fours and fives, filling the whole width of the road, and raising a dust, if there be the least dust to be raised, or making the mud fly in all directions; away they go, talking all together, while their horses are trotting at such a pace as one would think would shake the very teeth out of their heads.'

SEXY SALMON

'There is a theory ... that women tend to catch bigger fish than men do because their sexual scents – called pheromones – waft into the water and encourage the fish to bite. There is no doubt that fish have an astonishing sense of smell, salmon in particular being able to sense their way back to the river and often to the creek in which they were hatched. Experiments have shown that salmon become alarmed if a bear puts its paw in the water many yards upstream because they can detect the scent. Nevertheless, my husband, who is a former biologist, insists that the theory is rubbish, being based only on the fact that a few of the biggest salmon and trout caught in Britain have fallen to women. How, he asks, do the pheromones waft into the water from a woman encased up to the armpits in chest waders? And why should they attract only the big fish and fish of both sexes? He thinks that women owe their success either to luck or to being more patient, especially when fishing a salmon pool.'

From Tails And The Unexpected, A Collection of Unusual Angling Stories, *by Billee Chapman Pincher, published 1995 by Swan Hill Press*

• The theory that female sexual scents help women catch fish is backed up by the angling skills of the late Queen Mother, who aggravated male members of the Royal Family by regularly catching the largest salmon.

• A woman holds the record for the heaviest salmon ever caught in the British Isles. In 1922 Georgina Ballantyne landed a sixty-four pound fish on the Glendelvine stretch of the River Tay. Miss Ballantyne, who was in her twenties, was said to fish with such style that her father preferred to watch her cast rather than fish himself. Two years later another woman caught a sixty-one pound salmon on the Tay. However, the world's largest salmon was a monster of ninety-seven pounds caught in Alaska in 1985 – by a man.

RURAL REWARD

Each year tourists spend more than £2,000 million on trips to the English countryside.

TOO EXPENSIVE?

With supermarkets less interested in stocking expensive organic foods in recessionary times, the amount of UK land being converted to organic cultivation dropped by over 60 per cent from 2007 to 2010. In 2010 only 51,000 hectares were in 'conversion', the process farmers need to go through to have their land certified as organic – a marked decline from the 2007 organic peak of 158,000 hectares.

LOTTS OF PAINTING

THE MOST REPRODUCED VIEW of the English countryside is John Constable's 1821 painting *The Hay Wain*, a six-foot canvas that is classic chocolate box. Based on drawings made by Constable in Suffolk, near Flatford, on the River Stour, the picture was actually created in the artist's London studio.

The Hay Wain shows a horse-drawn hay cart standing in a river under dense clusters of clouds. The haymakers toil in the distance, across the meadow. On the left is a cottage that was rented by a farmer called Willy Lott. The building stands behind Flatford Mill, which was owned by Constable's father. The cottage and river are much today as they were in Constable's time, though the river runs deeper as East Anglia has sunk closer to sea level.

Constable's work was received more enthusiastically in France than at home, though he never ventured abroad. The French loved his nostalgic subject matter. A Parisian critic remarked: 'Constable paints nature at a point in history when its total destruction by the hand of man had not yet become conceivable. But only just …'

PAUSING ON EVERY CHARM

How often have I loitered o'er the green,
Where humble happiness endeared each scene!
How often have I paused on every charm,
The sheltered cot, the cultivated farm,
The never-failing brook, the busy mill,
The decent church that topped the neighbouring hill,
The hawthorn bush, with seats beneath the shade,
For talking age and whispering lovers made.

Oliver Goldsmith, from his masterpiece 'The Deserted Village', *1744*

Goldsmith mourned the simple rustic life that was being destroyed by the advancing agricultural revolution in which he saw rich landlords evicting peasants from the land and forcing them into industries such as coal mining.

NEW AGE MORONS

'PEOPLE IN THE COUNTRY ARE UNBEARABLY LAME. They dress either in hot, itchy tweed outfits or like New Age morons in gipsy skirts and waistcoats with CND badges. Everyone over 30 seems to have gaps between their misshapen, discoloured teeth. They fill their time buying junk at boot sales and making hideous pieces of trash they describe as "handicrafts" … They only bought their homes on a pretentious middleclass whim, inspired by some stupid lifestyle magazine, and are too proud to admit what a huge mistake they've made.'

Nirpal Dhaliwal, London Evening Standard

DUBIOUS SPORTS

'MUMBLE A SPARROW' was one of the more dubious games to be played at eighteenth-century country fairs. A sparrow with clipped wings was placed in the crown of a hat. The contestant, his arms tied behind him, attempted to bite off the sparrow's head. The pecks of the enraged bird usually ensured his defeat. Another barbarous sport went by the unfortunate name of 'whip the cock'. A cockerel was tied in a basket and half a dozen blindfolded farm boys with whips struck out at the bird, winning a prize if the creature cried out. They often ended up hitting each other, causing much merriment among the spectators.

> • Eighteenth-century Scottish country folk assembled annually in a field outside Kelso for an entertainment known as 'cat in a barrel'. A cat was stuffed into a barrel of soot and then the barrel was suspended on a crossbeam between two high poles. Men rode under the barrel and hit it with clubs until it broke. The idea was to dodge both falling soot and the extremely angry cat. The women and children would then zero in on the feline and, for no particular reason other than to have a good laugh, beat it to death. Such sport gave rise to the couplet: 'The cat in the barrel exhibits such a farce, That he who can relish it is worse than an ass.'

BARE

Some farmers say that you shouldn't plant potatoes until the soil is warm enough to sit on comfortably with your bare bottom.

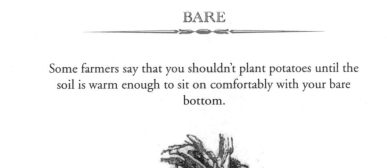

CAT TIP

A well-fed cat is better at hunting because it hunts for sport.
Because it is not hungry, it will watch the same spot for hours.
A starved cat eats the first thing it catches and then lies down to sleep.

BED OF WOOL

His bed of wool yields safe and quiet sleeps,
While by his side his faithful spouse hath place;
His little son into his bosom creeps,
The lively picture of his father's face:
Never his humble house nor state torment him;
Less he could like, if less his God had sent him!
And when he dies, green turfs, with grassy tomb, content him.

This description of the so-called perfect peasant life was by Thomas Fletcher (1666–1713), minor English poet and vicar

I.H.TREE

You plant pears
For your heirs.

Anon

ASK A SILLY QUESTION

'There are several different ways in which to lay out a little
garden; the best way is to get a gardener.'

Polish horticulturalist Karel Capek, from his 1931 manual The Gardener's Year

BRITAIN'S SUPERLATIVE TREES

Tallest tree in Britain is a 211-foot fir planted in the 1870s at Ardkinglas Woodland Gardens, beside Loch Fyne, Argyll, Scotland. In order to measure this monster, somebody climbed to the top and dropped a measuring tape to the ground. The tree achieved minor fame when it appeared in a 2003 episode of the BBC soap *EastEnders*: the drawing room at Ardkinglas House became the location for Barry's wedding before he met his end in Loch Fyne.

Thickest tree is a pedunculate oak at Fredville Park, near Dover, Kent. 'Majesty', as the tree is nicknamed, has a trunk thirteen feet across with a circumference of forty feet. It keeps this girth up to a height of about twenty feet; it is completely hollow.

Largest tree in volume is a sessile oak at Croft Castle, a National Trust property in Herefordshire. Described as Britain's biggest living thing, it is 115 feet tall with a trunk nine feet thick at its base, with a volume calculated at 3,800 cubic feet.

Oldest trees: three yews, all around 5,000 years old and all in churchyards – Fortinghall, Perthshire; Discoed, Powys; Llangernyw, Conwy – are thought to be the oldest living organisms in Europe. According to Scottish legend, Pontius Pilate was born in the shade of the Fortingall yew. Legend suggests that his father was a Roman official during the British occupation.

Rarest tree is the Audley End Oak (*Quercus audleyensis*), planted in 1772 at Audley End, Essex. All attempts to plant grafts have failed.

Most spreading tree is an Oriental plane planted in 1757 at Corsham Court in Wiltshire. It covers an area nearly the size of a football pitch, with a spread of more than 210 feet.

Fastest-growing tree was a silvertop eucalyptus at Harcourt Arboretum, Oxfordshire, which grew to sixty-six feet in six years. It died (of exhaustion?) in the winter of 2010.

AND ON A LESS CHEERFUL NOTE ...

Britain's most devastating tree diseases:

Sudden oak death: arrived in Britain in 2002 from America where it ravaged California's oak trees. In Britain the disease, *phytophthora ramorum*, has spared oaks and jumped to rhododendrons and Japanese larch. By 2011, some four million larch trees had been felled or marked for destruction. More are expected to be chopped down in the coming years as warmer, wetter conditions encourage the spread of the disease, a fungal condition that takes hold quickly, causing bleeding lesions, blackened or wilted leaves and, ultimately, death. Walkers in affected areas are urged to disinfect their boots to stop the disease spreading. No cure as yet.

Red band needle blight: affects Corsican pine; caused by the fungus *Dothistroma septosporum*. Results in needle defoliation, which may kill trees. The disease has increased dramatically over the past two decades owing to a rise in rainfall during spring and summer, coupled with warmer spring temperatures, which encourage spore dispersal and infection.

Bleeding canker, or horse chestnut disease: caused by the leaf miner moth, whose larvae eat the leaves. This causes a dark liquid to ooze from spots on the trunk. These quickly develop into large damaged patches, spreading all the way around the trunk until limbs fall off, or the tree falls over. Discovered in Britain in 2006, it quickly spread to around 10 per cent of all horse chestnuts. Since branches tend to drop off weakened trees, safety concerns have meant that thousands in urban streets have been cut down. Scientists are trying to find a cure.

Dutch elm disease: an old enemy that affects the UK's main elm tree species including the English Elm (*Ulmus procera*), Wych Elm (*Ulmus glabra*) and the Smooth Leaved Elm (*Ulmus minor*). The fungus is transmitted by two European bark beetles: the large beetle *Scolytus scolytus*; and the small elm bark beetle *Scolytus multistriatus*. Fungal spores stick to the beetles and are introduced to the tree when the creatures bore into the bark to feed. The fungus infects the tree's vascular system and eventually the tree wilts and dies. The first outbreak was in the Netherlands in 1910; it spread to the UK in the 1920s and has been rife in Britain since the late 1960s, thanks to a more aggressive fungus known as *Ophiostoma novo-ulmi*. In late summer the effects of DED can be seen in hedgerows as leaves on young elm trees turn prematurely brown and yellow and wilt. The Forestry Commission advises us to conserve British elms by keeping them trimmed. Larger trees are more likely to attract bark beetles. Washing boots and vehicle wheels can prevent the disease from spreading.

FECKING FRECKLES

NINETEENTH-CENTURY COUNTRY GENTLEFOLK considered that suntans were 'common', but freckles were worse. Freckles meant you had spent your life toiling outdoors, which was considered most unfortunate in a lady. Thus the Victorians spent much time concocting recipes for removing such facial disfigurements. *Golden Rule* magazine of the 1840s published this guidance:

'To Remove Freckles. Freckles are occasioned by exposure to heat, and give to the complexion a very disagreeable appearance; they are removed by the following applications, the surface of the skin having been previously softened by a little mild balsam or emollient paste.

Freckle Paste:
One ounce of bitter almonds, one ounce of barley flour. Mix with a sufficient quantity of honey to make the whole into a smooth paste, with which the face, particularly where freckles appear, is to be anointed at night, and the paste washed off in the morning.

Freckle Wash:
Take one drachm of muriatic acid, half a pint of rain water, half a teaspoonful of spirit of lavender. Mix them well together, and apply two or three times a day to the freckles with a camel's hair brush.

Lemon Cream For Sunburn And Freckles:
Put two spoonfuls of fresh cream into half a pint of new milk; squeeze into it the juice of a lemon, and half a pint of brandy, a little alum, and loaf sugar; boil the whole, skim well, and when cool, it is fit for use.'

Note: the Victorian theory that lemon juice removed freckles was disproved years ago.

BRANDISHING A DILDO

THE WOMEN'S INSTITUTE, bastion of rural correctness, raised eyebrows in 2008 with the launch of a video designed to help members improve their sex lives. Tips included the best sexual position to adopt if your husband suffered from arthritis or heart problems. And in case he couldn't raise a smile in the first place, there was a guide to the most efficient battery-operated sex aids.

Presenter Janice Langley, 66, was a retired sex therapist and member of Washington W.I. in West Sussex. Reclining on a bed with a variety of top-shelf magazines and dodgy DVDs, she brandished a dildo telling viewers, 'They come in all shapes and sizes. You may say nice girls don't do that, but they do and they enjoy it.' She proceeded to recommend 'doing it' in the drawing room, the kitchen and the garden.

'We have a diverse membership', Mrs Langley commented. 'We're not all eighty-five and knitting.'

The Women's Institute was formed in 1915 during the First World War to revitalise rural communities and to encourage women to produce food. By the beginning of the twenty-first century it was still the largest women's organisation in the UK with over 200,000 members in 6,500 branches.

SOCIAL GENIUS

'Of all the great things that the English have invented and made a part of the credit of the national character, the most perfect, the most characteristic, the one they have mastered most completely in all its details, so that it has become a compendious illustration of their social genius and their manners, is the well-appointed, well-filled country house.'

American-born writer Henry James (1843–1916)

WORSE NOT BETTER

In some rural parts of the North of England it is considered unlucky
for a bride to marry a man whose surname begins
with the same initial as hers:

'If you change the name, and not the letter,
You change for the worse, and not the better.'

• A bride who marries a man with the same surname will become expert at
baking bread, or so they say.

IRRESISTIBLE

'All the evidence ... suggests that there is a force deep in the English psyche
which is driving people to aspire to a rural lifestyle. Unlike Americans who
strive for a suburban lifestyle, for the British the lure of the countryside seems
more irresistible than ever.'

Professor Tony Champion of Newcastle University's geography department

PERFECT SHADE

'No tree has more comfortable roots for the weary to rest upon than
the beech. Often beech roots rise high out of the ground, and are
twisted about to form seats of all shapes. And beech trees are
very cool to sit beneath, as their leaves most perfectly
shade the ground beneath from sunlight.'

*From a chapter charmingly titled 'The Art of Sitting Down'
which appears in a book called* Ways and Secrets of
the True Countryman, *by O. Jones and
M. Woodward, published in
the early 1900s*

ASPIRATIONAL

A DOZEN WINES that should be found in the cellar of any self-respecting country house:

1. **Pol Roger Brut Réserve Champagne:** Winston Churchill drank Pol Roger, the 1928 being his favourite. Pol Roger was drunk at the Duke and Duchess of Cambridge's wedding. The Brut Réserve or 'White Foil', as it is commonly known, is one of the most consistent of the 'grande marque' champagnes; a classic choice for any country house cellar and it won't hurt if it is forgotten for a year or two to mature further.

2. **Mâcon-Chardonnay, Talmard.** Chilean Sauvignon and Chardonnay that is drinking a little above its station; useful stand-by for lunch or dinner.

3. **Jackson Estate 'Green Lip' Sauvignon Blanc, Marlborough, New Zealand.** A fine example of the Kiwis beating the French at their own game; sort of turbo-charged Sancerre. Good with fish.

4. **Meursault, Clos de la Barre, Domaine des Comtes Lafon.** For serious dinner parties, it is hard to beat a well-cellared white Burgundy from Meursault or Puligny-Montrachet. One can serve a more complex, minerally premier cru if guests appreciate it, but a straight 'village' wine from a top grower normally satisfies the squire's palate. You can also try Coche-Dury, Leflaive, Henri Germain, Carillon, Pierre Morey, Ramonet and assorted members of the Pillot family. These are wines made from Chardonnay vines grown on limestone slopes below wild boar-infested oak forests. The wines take two to three years to knit together and can be left for up to thirty years, though old white Burgundy is an acquired taste. Goes well with oysters.

5. **Sancerre Rosé, André Dezat et Fils.** Rosé has finally shaken off its shocking reputation gained in the 1970s with aberrations such as Mateus. It would be a shame not to have some good dry rosé for those summer lunches on the terrace. Sancerre from the eastern end of the Loire valley is worth seeking out.

6. **Château Léoville-Barton, 2me cru Saint-Julien 1982.** Anthony Barton is the epitome of the Anglo-Irishman abroad, residing in the Haut-Médoc in the beautiful Château Langoa-Barton which his family has owned since 1821. The cellars for both Langoa and its more famous second growth stablemate, Léoville-Barton, are across the road with much of the operation now run by Anthony's daughter, Lillian Sartorius-Barton. Wise British buyers regularly put a case or two of Léoville-Barton and Langoa in their cellars. Exceptional vintages are 1982, 1985, 1986, 1989, 1990, while the 1966 and 1961, even though aged, still drink marvellously. Anthony and Lillian maintain a sensible un-Parisian

attitude to pricing, preferring long-term relationships to short-term profiteering.

7. **Châteauneuf-du-Pape, Domaine du Vieux Télégraphe 1998.** In 1898 Hippolyte Brunier planted his first vines on the Crau plateau. The estate takes its name from the tower on the hillside which was used as a telegraph station. The 1978 vintage is legendary, but the 1998 is also excellent, exhibiting all the herby nuances of the South of France.

8. **Viña Real Reserva Rioja, CVNE 2005.** Since the late 1970s, Rioja has been the obvious alternative to mature claret. There are many good houses alongside CVNE, such as La Rioja Alta, Marques de Murrieta, Marques de Caceres, Conterno, Lopez Heredia and Tobelos. Note: gold wire wrapped around a Rioja bottle was originally a deterrent to tampering and, more recently, a sign of quality, but should be treated with circumspection these days as it is probably more of a marketing gimmick.

9. **Château Rieussec 1er cru Sauternes 1990.** A truly great pudding wine. Since 1984 Château Rieussec has been owned by the Rothschild family of Château Lafite fame. Its 90 hectares of vines are spread over the hillsides of the communes of Fargues and Sauternes, making them perfectly placed for the morning fogs which are crucial for the development of the noble rot needed to make this type of sweet wine. Classic years are 1961, 1971, 1975, 1983, 1986, 1988, 1990 and 2001. The French drink Sauternes while they pig out on foie gras, but the English know that Sauternes goes best with lemon tart or crème brûlée.

10. **Manzanilla La Gitana, Bodegas Hidalgo.** Javier Hidalgo, chairman of Bodegas Hidalgo, is a great Anglophile and has been a regular on the English hunting field since the 1980s. This is the perfect tapas sherry which should be drunk with stuffed olives, salted almonds and slivers of Jamón Ibérico; but can cope with anything from devilled chicken to curried eggs.

11. **Graham's 20-year-old Tawny Port.** One of the greatest names of port, Graham's was formerly a textile business in Oporto. In 1970 it was bought by the Anglo-Portuguese Symington family, which owns rival brands Dow's and Warre's. Tawny port is lighter than Late Bottled Vintage or Vintage, and is best served chilled.

12. **Taylor's Vintage Port 1963.** The granddaddy of the country house cellar. Taylor's achieves the highest prices for its ports. Deservedly so when one looks back at an array of stellar vintages such as 1945, 1948, 1955, 1960, 1963, 1966, 1970, 1977 and 1980. The desert island wine for many would be the 1963, which has a perfect poise of sweet, mature, complex fruit and spirit.

With thanks to Tanners of Shrewsbury, Shropshire, vintners to the landed gentry. Proprietor James Tanner warns: 'Some of these wines are quite aspirational. They are certainly not to be demolished by teenagers.'

YEARNING FOR THE OLD FARM

An idyllic and highly optimistic early Victorian view of English country life:

'How dear to every English heart is the old farm! The very name is a household word amongst us. Like "home" and "family", it is one of those expressions which claim affinity with our most cherished feelings … the farm is a part of ourselves, and its mention recalls a thousand pleasant associations. The poor shop-boy who can speak of his "grandfather's farm", holds his head proudly above his fellows. Should he live to ride in the Lord Mayor's coach, he will never be ashamed of "the farm", nor of "old dobbin", albeit he remembers well that the poor animal's protruding bones betrayed his owner's poverty.

'In yonder senate the veteran statesman lays out the plan of a parliamentary campaign, and devotes himself to sleepless nights and days of incessant labour, as if he loved the toil better than all else on earth. But he is an Englishman, and "home" is nearer to his heart than glory; his early life was spent in the country, and "the farm" holds the next place in his heart to home.

'The merchant is resolutely bent on enriching his children. Yet dearer than riches to his heart is the thought of the farm he means to purchase, "when his ship comes home". And the children! how they talk of the cows, and the new milk; the sheep and the poultry; the ponies they will ride, and the glorious haymaking they will have!

'The mechanic in the midst of his toil loves to think of the farm. He remembers his weary walk from a distant town, and the farmhouse at which he obtained a draught of sweet milk from the cow, such as he has never tasted since. His thoughts, night and day, are of farming. He will go a voyage further than Jason travelled for the Golden Fleece, that he may possess a little farm of his own before he dies, and leave an inheritance in land to his children.

'That poor slattern – wretched as she looks, and wretched as is the murky den, in the warren of courts and alleys, which she calls her home – cherishes one bright remembrance of her youthful days. It is the memory of the farmhouse where she first went into service, and the meadows through which she went singing on her simple errands.

'There is enchantment in the first view of the old farm to the weary traveller, returning, after his long journey through life's rough road, to the home of his childhood – the geese that hiss with outstretched necks as he passes through their midst and the pig that rolls out of his path with a lazy grunt, seem to him the very same that he left there thirty years before. Generations pass by, and the old homestead is but little altered. It is hardly an exaggeration to say, that the old farm, like the hills and woods, is a part of the harmony of Nature.'

The Traveller's Album, *published London 1842*

FRESHNESS BREATHES

Now from the town
Buried in smoke, and sleep, and noisome damps,
Oft let me wander o'er the dewy fields,
Where freshness breathes, and dash the trembling drops
From the bent bush, as through the verdant maze
Of sweet-briar hedges I pursue my walk.

Scottish poet James Thomson (1700–1748), from his
masterpiece 'The Seasons'

FRUIT FACT

A 100-year-old pear tree can yield a ton of pears a year.

DOLLY MUTTON

MOST FAMOUS SHEEP IN HISTORY, with the possible exception of the lambs who attended the birth of Christ, is Dolly, the world's first cloned mammal.

Dolly became a scientific sensation when she was born on 5th July, 1996, at the Roslin Institute, Edinburgh. The cell used for the cloning of Dolly was taken from the mammary gland of a six-year-old Finn Dorset ewe. Dolly was named after the American country singer Dolly Parton. Professor Sir Ian Wilmut, embryologist in charge of the project, explained, 'We couldn't think of a more impressive pair of mammary glands.'

Dolly lived all her life at Roslin. She bred with a Welsh Mountain ram and produced six lambs. However, she was plagued with arthritis and died aged 7 from lung disease – a Dorset should live to about 12. The Roslin scientists denied that Dolly's early demise was a result of her being cloned but critics speculated that she was born with a genetic age of 6, the same age as the sheep from whence she came.

• In 2010 it was revealed that Dolly herself had been cloned. Four of her exact genetic copies – nicknamed 'The Dollies' – were alive and well and gambolling in a field at Nottingham University.

• Welsh farmer Iolo Owen has spent years creating the 'perfect' sheep called the Easy Care, a revolutionary breed that requires minimal shepherding yet offers excellent meat yields and lambing ratios. Easy Care sheep can lamb outside with no need for a shepherd and have wiry coats that do not need shearing. The animals require minimal treatment for fly strike and are less likely to become stuck on their backs.

COLDEST DAY

THE COLDEST DAY OF THE YEAR is traditionally St Hilary's Day, 13th January. One of the most severe winters in history began on 13th January, 1205: the River Thames froze over in London; ale froze solid and had to be sold by weight. The freeze lasted until 20th March. St Hilary was a fourth-century French bishop.

HUMAN SQUIRREL

ADVICE ON CLIMBING TREES from *Games And Sports For Young Boys*, published by Routledge, Warne and Routledge, 1859:

'Summer is the proper time for practising this recreation, as the withered boughs may then be easily detected, and even then, until some experience has been purchased at the expense of a few mishaps, it is the best plan to climb low, stunted trees. The kind of wood and strength of the branches must always be especially considered; and as the surface of the branches is either smooth, or moist and slippery, the grasp should never be relaxed for an instant. By practice, the climber becomes so expert that when the branches hang tolerably low, instead of scrambling up the trunk of the tree, by taking a short run and a spring, he may seize a branch, swing himself up, and then proceed from bough to bough, or even from tree to tree, should they be planted close enough.'

FOR OUR MORE RUGGED COUNTRYMEN

Rules for tossing the caber:

The caber is a tapered wooden pole, anywhere from sixteen to twenty-two feet long, weighing between a hundred and a hundred and eighty pounds. The smaller end of the pole is cradled in the palms of the thrower's clasped hands and the weight of it is balanced against their shoulder. The thrower runs forward for twenty yards or so, increasing speed to gain momentum. Then he tosses the pole by pushing upward and letting it fall forward from the shoulder. Contrary to popular belief, the distance of the toss is irrelevant. The judges observe the angle that the caber falls in relation to the thrower's shoulders. The winner is judged on style of throwing as well as strength, balance and agility.

• In the American Highland Games rules, the caber toss is judged on the distance thrown making it a far more competitive (and, dare one say it, more interesting) sport.

• Tartan trivia: what should be worn under a kilt? The regulations of the Scottish Official Board of Highland Dancing state that underpants should be worn. They should be dark coloured, never white. The practice of eschewing underwear is sometimes referred to as 'going regimental' or 'going commando'. There is no official British Army policy regarding this.

SHEEP DOG

'You must not shear the sheep of its wool
Before the dog-rose is at the full.'

Old country saying

A LOVELY GIFT FOR A BISHOP

How to make the perfect hazel walking stick, or shepherd's crook:

'Cut a rod in winter, selecting one that has the appropriate shape for a handle, and of a length suitable for the eventual user. Do not peel but leave to season for six months. When the process is complete the bark will come away easily. Shape the handle with a file and sandpaper, and then likewise the rest of the surfaces. Make several applications of furniture polish, buffing between each until the stick is coppery in colour. A really good crook would be a lovely gift for a bishop.'

From Thorn, Fire and Lily: Gardening with God in Lent and Easter
by Jane Mossendew, published by Burns and Oates, 2004

Folklore records hazel as being a highly powerful wood. In Somerset people stirred jam with a hazel twig to prevent fairies stealing it. It is said that hazel creates a chemical reaction that prevents jam from shrinking.

• A curious 1867 work with the splendid title *Notes And Studies In The Philosophy of Animal Magnetism and Spiritualism With Observations Upon Catarrh, Bronchitis, Rheumatism, Gout, Scrofula, And Cognate Diseases,* claimed that hazel possessed mild magnetic qualities that could affect sleep-walkers: 'A stick cut from a hazel tree … exhibits two opposite poles. Among the striking facts appertaining to the hazel stick are some very curious phenomena. If a highly sensitive sleep-walker has a hazel stick held at a certain short distance from the face perpendicularly, in the direction of its growth, the individual will be attracted towards it. If, on the other hand, the stick be held in the direction contrary to its growth, that is to say with its tapering end downwards, the individual will be repelled from the stick.'

The author of *Notes and Studies etc.* was John Ashburner (1793–1878), a member of the Royal College of Surgeons, who has been described as a physician, physicist, phrenologist, mesmerist and spiritualist.

• Cultivated hazelnuts called filberts take their name from St Philibert's Day, 20th August, the date on which hazelnuts are supposed to start ripening.

FATAL FARMS

BRITISH AGRICULTURE has one of the worst accident records of any employment sector in the UK. From 1998 to 2008 there were 461 fatal accidents within the farming industry, an average of almost one a week. Figures for 2008-09 revealed that 26 workers were killed and another 589 suffered major injuries in farming accidents.

While farming accounts for only 1.7 per cent of the UK workforce, it is responsible for nearly 20 per cent of worker fatalities. The Health and Safety Executive say that, unlike other industries, there has been no decline in farming accidents during the first decade of the current century. Of the 461 people killed over the past ten years, 145 were employees, 251 were self-employed, and 65 were members of the public, of whom 26 were children under the age of 16.

The most common causes of UK farming accidents:

1. Farm vehicles – tractors, combine harvesters, diggers and quad bikes cause a quarter of all farm injuries.
2. Falls from height, especially roofs, lofts, trees and ladders.
3. Livestock. Cows and bulls can be large and unpredictable.

4. Falling objects including bales of hay, bits of wood, masonry, trees.
5. Burn injuries from hot machinery and naked flames.
6. Asphyxiation and drowning in grainage silos and slurry pits; surprisingly high at 10 per cent of all farming deaths 1998–2008.
7. Accidents with machinery – fork lifts, conveyor belts, baling machines.
8. Electric shocks.
9. Poisoning.
10. Gassing.

A 2008 survey showed that 18,000 people in the agriculture industry suffered from an illness which was caused or made worse by their job. Long-term killers include 'farmer's lung', a respiratory disorder caused by dust and pesticide inhalation. Asbestos is often found in farm buildings, leading to cancers such as mesothelioma. Loud machinery can cause hearing loss. Long-term use of vibrating tools can result in nerve damage.

The HSE predict that, over the next decade, farm injuries are likely to increase thanks to the growing numbers of small agricultural contractors who are less likely to take health and safety as seriously as larger farming operations. Changes in weather patterns, including heavier winter rain, may lead farmers to cut corners and take greater risks in order to maximise profits.

• Certain hay balers can be terrifyingly dangerous. There are countless examples of people suffering injuries from these machines, notably five women in New York State, who were scalped and suffered severe facial disfigurement as a result of their hair becoming entangled in drive shafts. Such accidents have led to improved shielding on drive shafts and other moving parts.

• James Chapman, elected chairman of the National Federation of Young Farmers' Clubs (NFYFC) in 2010, became a victim of bad farm safety when he lost his arm in an unguarded PTO shaft: 'I was under pressure to finish a job and had an accident which has changed my life forever.' The NFYFC, which has 23,000 members, has been running a campaign to improve farm safety.

YESTERDAY ...

'IF I WERE EVEN TO CONTEMPLATE TELLING MY READERS that I knew why and wherefore salmon rose from the depths of the water and seized upon what are called salmon-flies, I should consider myself meditating an arch-deception. … A dissertation to prove why salmon took one artificial fly, and rejected another, which other salmon afterwards very willingly take, would just be as sensible and profitable as that referring to the angels—fairies if you will—and the needle's point. Many an hour do I pass in speculative surprise and open-mouthed wonderment, for there is nothing that astonishes me more than the effects of a salmon-fly manoeuvred after a certain fashion through the waters of a salmon-river.'

The Book of the Salmon
by Edward Fitzgibbon, 1850

... AND TODAY

'THE SEA-RUN ATLANTIC SALMON is an extraordinary fish. Large and classically proportioned, during its relatively short life it bestrides the two very different worlds of fresh and salt water. Its migrations far into northern seas to grow and subsequent return to its place of birth to breed are nothing less than heroic, and that return, with its dramatic leaps at falls, offers a wildlife spectacle no other fish can match. Its presence – or its absence – is a vital indicator of the relative health of our rivers and seas. Over the millennia, it has accrued totemic as well as culinary importance to the societies that caught it and for most of the last one it has enjoyed the conservation benefits of laws carefully drafted to protect it. Down the long years, the ancient statutes and their successors kept the great fish safe until, over little more than two centuries, first the rivers and estuaries and finally even the seas themselves, fell foul of industrial man's capacity to plunder the priceless resources he had inherited. For the first time in its long evolutionary history, the survival of the Atlantic salmon as a species can no longer be taken for granted. Many populations have been lost or put at risk, but the enduring power of this remarkable fish to capture the imagination of naturalists and sportsmen has so far proved a sure shield against its extinction.'

From To Sea and Back, The Heroic Life of the Atlantic Salmon, *by Richard Shelton, published 2009 by Atlantic Books. Shelton is Research Director of the Atlantic Salmon Trust*

LAST EARTHLY PILGRIMAGE

'The passage through a country house of the framed photograph of a friend is often an instructive spectacle to witness. Such a trophy usually begins its career in the drawing room. It is then moved to the library, and subsequently to the smoking room. After that it begins a heavenly flight into one of the guest rooms, from which place it ascends on its last earthly pilgrimage to the attic.'

Francis W. Croninshield,
Manners For The Metropolis, *1909*

AN ABOMINABLY BAD SERMON

Renowned Victorian country parson Andrew Boyd on the subject of sermons:

'The writing of sermons does you good. However, in preaching your sermons you are somewhat annoyed by rustic boorishness and want of thought. Various bumpkins will forget to close the door behind them when they enter church too late. Various men with great hob-nailed shoes will stamp noisily up the passage to the further extremity of the church. Various faces will look up at you week by week, hopelessly blank of all interest or intelligence. Some human beings will not merely sleep, but loudly evince that they are sleeping. You gradually cease to be worried by these little things. At first, they jarred through every nerve; but you grow accustomed to them. And if you be a man of principle and of sense, you know better than to fancy that amid a rustic people your powers are thrown away. ... I have no patience with men who preach sermons carelessly prepared because they have an uneducated congregation. Nowhere is more careful preparation needed; but of course it must be preparation of the right sort. Let it be received as an axiom, that the very first aim of the preacher should be to interest. He must interest, before he can hope to instruct or improve. And no matter how filled with orthodox doctrine and good advice a sermon may be: if it put the congregation to sleep, it is an abominably bad sermon.'

PURRANORMAL

Little excites country folk more than talk of wild cat sightings. Ever since the British wolf became extinct in the eighteenth century people have looked for another bogeyman upon which to blame mutilated sheep, etc.

Hundreds of big cats are said to roam the kingdom, with numerous so-called sightings, though curiously there has been remarkably little evidence to back them up. From 2005 to 2010 there were more than forty sightings of big cats in the UK. Even the government body Natural England believes in them: 'The evidence is there that there are the odd, escaped, released, dumped animals occurring in the wild every now and then. Believing in big cats is not like believing in the Loch Ness monster. There is absolutely no doubt that they are out there.'

Such evidence includes a roe deer in Surrey that had been dragged over two fences, ripped apart and left with puncture marks that could have come from a large cat. Meanwhile, a strange, purring creature spotted by a roadside in Somerset was said to be as tall as a car.

Wales claims a fair proportion of UK 'big cats', including panthers, though not one has been produced for public examination. Recent sightings include:

A tiger on a bridge over the M4.

A black panther and two cubs in Troedyrhiw.

A cat the size of a Labrador with lynx-like ears mucking about by the light of a Carmarthen street lamp.

A giant puma lurking in a garden in the Vale of Glamorgan (pumas are always 'giant'; you never hear of normal-sized pumas).

In Carmarthen, a farmer described discovering large panther-like paw prints on a cycle path, saying he had 'never seen anything like it' in his life.

• As if to prove a national obsession with big cats, there are endless UK organisations devoted to the subject, notably the British Big Cats Society, Big Cats In Britain, bigcatmonitors.co.uk, UK Big Cats and Big Cats GB.

• In 2010 wildlife film maker Mark Fletcher claimed there was a government conspiracy to cover up big cat sightings. Fletcher, who was making a documentary about British big cats, told of huge road kill being removed by police. He alleged that Defra and others were afraid that Freedom of Information requests would reveal more than they wanted to admit. Families of leopards were living in the Forest of Dean, but a local Wildlife Trust employee had ordered him to keep mum so that the cats would not be disturbed. 'It's certainly in the interests of the authorities to keep the truth under lock and key', Fletcher said. 'Leopards and lynxes are alien and potentially dangerous. If their presence is confirmed, Natural England and Defra may have to spend valuable time and money finding and culling them. This would be both difficult and controversial.' Not half: Defra have enough difficulty coping with badgers without having to worry about leopards.

• How to deal with that big cat when you finally meet it: as with most aggressive animals, don't turn your back and run off. Even tigers do not like to attack head-on. Slowly back away, keeping a face-on view of the cat at all times. Also, it would be helpful if you could remember to take a photograph. Having done that, run like hell.

• Visitors to Wales should look out for werewolves which are prevalent in the principality, or so they say. It started back in 1790 when a stagecoach travelling between Denbigh and Wrexham was overturned and the occupants ripped to pieces by an enormous black beast almost as long as the coach horses. Naturally it was a full moon. In February 1992 a bear-like creature was spotted in North Wales on the night of a full moon. Two lambs were subsequently found savaged.

• The village of Brymbo, North Wales, was terrorised in 1985 by a half-man half-animal with smoking nostrils prowling the streets at night. A terrified local woman reported: 'It just stood there, frowning down at us with its eyes wrinkled up. Its hooves were sort of dangling down in front of it.' In the pub later they reached the conclusion that it was probably some bloke having a fag while dressed in a cow costume.

PUTTING THE CHEST INTO CHESTER

THE POSHEST RACE DAYS IN BRITAIN (as compiled by a select and not entirely sober group of the author's racing friends):

1. **Glorious Goodwood (July).** Edward VII called it 'a garden party with racing tacked on'. All five days are achingly nobby and the racing is top-notch. Blessedly few Ascot riff-raff.

2. **Gold Cup day, Cheltenham (March).** The landed gentry and the cream of the Shires descend on Cheltenham to join forces with Ireland's punters for the year's finest racing over jumps. Like a huge point-to-point. Gold Cup day is a must, as long as you can tolerate the traffic jams upon departure.

3. **Tuesday of Royal Ascot (June).** Best racing of the week. Quite different from the other days when the Royal Enclosure is crammed with tottering harpies in hats, many of them sporting tattoos done in unguarded moments on holidays in Faliraki.

4. **Ebor Meeting, York (August).** The Ebor Festival is a historic race meeting founded in 1843 to amuse the northern aristocracy. Top-class racing in a beautiful setting. Extremely social.

5. **Grand National day, Aintree (April).** Enough fizz-quaffing nobs to detract from the beer 'n' skittles.

6. **Cartmel: The Burlington Slate Grand Veterans National day (May/June)** is gratifyingly upmarket. National Hunt racing in its most original format. Cartmel is a small racecourse in Cumbria on a private estate. Beautifully understated, packed with local toffs. [Note: Cartmel is of great sentimental value to punters because of the legendary 1974 Gay Future attempted betting coup. An Irish trainer (subsequently convicted for fraud) had soap flakes rubbed into a horse's coat to make it look as though it was sweating, thus persuading punters not to put their money on it and thereby increasing the odds.]

7. **The Craven Meeting, Newmarket (April).** First decent flat meeting of the season and a relief for racegoers looking for a break from jumping (although some say that such people are beyond the pale and should be fed to the hounds).

8. **City of Perth Gold Cup, Perth (April).** Northernmost track in Britain. Members Enclosure is restrained and tweedy.

9. **Ladies' Day, May Festival, Chester (May).** Charmingly urban but enough gentry to save the day. The finest totty to be seen at any racecourse in the country. Puts the 'chest' into Chester.

10. **Prix de l'Arc de Triomphe, Longchamp (October).** Okay, so it's not in Britain but the meeting seems to attract more English racegoers than French. (Perhaps this is because French courses don't rip off racegoers.) We may have lost Calais but there is a corner of France that is forever England.

SLOW MISTLETOE

How to grow your own mistletoe:

1. Choose your host tree. Half the mistletoe grown in England grows on apple trees, undoubtedly the best. But poplar, lime and hawthorn can work reasonably well. Remember that mistletoe is a parasite and will reduce fruit yield on an apple tree.

2. Obtain some berries. It's best to harvest them fresh in February – mistletoe berries cut at Christmas are not ideal. If the berries have been stored, rehydrate them for a few hours in water. Fresh or stored, the seed needs to be squeezed out of the berry, along with a quantity of the sticky viscin. Collect several sticky seeds on your fingers.

3. Stick the seeds onto a young branch, about an inch or two in diameter. Avoid older branches and the trunk. Label the branch. Plant as many seeds as possible, the contents of at least twenty berries at once, divided between four or five branches. Many seeds will die, or be eaten by birds.

4. By March–April your surviving seeds should be germinating. Mistletoe is very slow. You will not see any leaf for three years. After the third year the mistletoe plant will start growing rapidly.

RELATIVELY ORDINARY

IN THE EARLY 1980s a term sprung up to describe the new generation of urbanites moving to the countryside in order to work part-time from home. They were known as 'Droppies' – Disillusioned, Relatively Ordinary Professionals, Preferring Independent Employment Situations. The 1991 census revealed that 250,000 people, fed up with gridlocked traffic and the prospect of negative housing equity, sold their town properties in order to pursue a rural lifestyle. One social observer noted drily, 'Being a Droppie in the Eighties carried with it a certain idealism. Droppies ran smallholdings breeding ostriches or wild boar. They got on to village committees and wrote it all up in *Country Living* or *The Guardian*.'

A GRATIFYING SIGHT TO A REFLECTING MIND

Nineteenth-century sporting writer Charles Apperley, aka 'Nimrod', explains the mechanics of the plough:

'How simple does the action of the plough appear to be. Only three things are to be performed:

- a slice of earth is cut off from the general mass;
- this slice is removed some inches to one side;
- the slice of earth is so turned that it may expose a new surface to the air, and what was formerly uppermost may now be undermost or buried.

To the performance of these things the construction of the plough must be adapted, and the work must be done with as little labour to the ploughman as possible. He must have it in his power to vary, at pleasure, the depth, width, and position of the furrow. The first of these actions is performed by the coulter, the second and third by the sock and moulboard jointly, and it is by the position of these parts, together with the form of the beam which governs the draught, that a good or bad plough is produced.'

Apperley had a thing about ploughmen. Echoing Cicero's assertion that 'nothing is more beautiful than a well-cultivated field', Apperley added dreamily: 'To see a well-grown young Englishman walking between the stilts of his plough with a free step and an erect body, with both horses and plough quite under his command, is a gratifying sight to a reflecting mind.'

From The Oracle of Rural Life, An Almanack For Sportsmen, Farmers, Gardeners and Country Gentlemen, *1839*

• Ploughing excited many nineteenth-century authors. Garden and landscape writer John Loudon declared that ploughing could be as thrilling as hunting or shooting: 'The occasional holding of the plough is an operation which calls into moderate exercise every part of the body, and which also engages the mind in keeping the furrow straight. We speak from experience, when we say that we consider this the most agreeable of all farming operations, and one by which a maximum of exercise may be obtained with a minimum of fatigue. The handles of the plough, draw, as it were, the operator after it, and the necessity of keeping his eye on two points, seen through between the pair of horses, occupies his attention. The occupation of ploughing with two horses is a light exercise for a gentleman and a philosopher; and we can readily conceive the country gentlemen of Britain, at some future time, substituting this, and other agricultural labours, for the sports of the field.'

• The greatest advance in ploughing arrived in the 1850s with the invention of John Fowler's steam plough. Yorkshireman Fowler (1826–1864) was an agricultural engineer whose inventions reduced the cost of ploughing farmland, and also enabled the drainage of previously uncultivated land. While on a trip to Ireland, Fowler realised that much of the land was uncultivated because it was waterlogged. He returned to England to develop a horse-powered ploughing engine that would dig drainage channels. His plough was pulled across a field on ropes driven by horses that walked round a capstan. Two years later the horses were replaced with a steam engine. In 1854, and after many changes to his design, Fowler produced a machine that could plough an acre an hour. By 1860 Fowler's ploughs were being sold all over the world. It was a classic success story of the Industrial Revolution.

Fowler's wealth enabled him to retire early to a West Yorkshire estate where he took up hunting. At the age of 38 he became yet another victim of this dangerous sport when he fell while out with the Badsworth. He sustained a compound fracture of his arm and died a day later from tetanus.

• The day on which work started after Twelfth Night was known as Plough Monday because this was when labourers had to return to the fields.

QUIRKY COUNTRY LADY

'Science, or para-science, tells us that geraniums bloom better if they are spoken to. But a kind word every now and then is really quite enough. Too much attention, like too much feeding, and weeding and hoeing, inhibits and embarrasses them.'

British author Victoria Glendinning

TRUFFLE TROVE

With English truffles fetching more than £200 a kilo you can train your dog to find truffles in the woods.

Here are a few tips:

- Dedicate fifteen minutes a day to training. Always reward the dog if he finds something.

- Start by throwing a piece of cheese onto bare ground and teaching Fido to find it.

- Then hide the cheese in the ground and train him to find it.

- Thirdly, place a truffle under the buried piece of cheese and get the dog used to the scent.

- The fourth stage is to hide the truffle without including a piece of cheese. The dog will locate the truffle, but then go and find the cheese instead and dig that up.

- Finally, put the cheese on top of the truffle but insist that the dog digs up the truffle. When the dog has mastered this, hide the truffle without the cheese and again, insist that the dog digs it up. Reward with cheese from your pocket.

Truffles grow across Britain but they take a lot of finding. The classic English truffle – *Tuber aestivum* – is the size of a small apple, black and veined with white inside. It grows from July until winter and can be found around the roots of beech, oak and birch. It is a much sought-after delicacy, although it does not possess the cachet of its French cousin, the black Perigord (*Tuber melanosporum*).

• Truffle hunters in both the UK and France keep their finds as secret as possible. It is suspected that French *truffiers* release only a small proportion of their finds onto the market in order to keep prices high – at the turn of the nineteenth century the French were harvesting around 1,000 tonnes annually whereas the haul is barely twenty tonnes today.

• Much to the irritation of the French, UK truffle hunters claim that the world's greatest concentration of the fungi lies in woodland on the Berkshire-Wiltshire borders.

• The French sometimes use pigs to hunt for truffles. Pigs have better noses than dogs, but they are more difficult to control.

SHOOT THE BUGGER

The racing trainer's excuses ... and what the owner is really thinking:

'He's a bit short of a run.'	('He's a tub of lard.')
'Track was a bit tight.'	('Jockey seemed tight to me.')
'He's a bit lazy.'	('He's bone idle.')
'He got hemmed in.'	('Jockey needs a bollocking.')
'He was very unlucky.'	('Weren't we all?')
'He swallowed his tongue.'	('Wish I'd swallowed mine before I backed him each way.')
'Might try blinkers next time.'	('Face facts, you've bought a camel.')
'Thought he would win until the final furlong.'	('He'd lost before he left the paddock.')
'Going well until the last.'	('Never stood a chance.')
'He'll strip fitter next time.'	('Trust in the power of prayer.')
'Hasn't found his form.'	('Shoot the bugger.')

From a booklet with contributions from the racing world, published in the 1990s to raise funds for the Spinal Injuries Association.

• 'When I see a trainer over polite to his owner friends, begging them to indulge in yet more champagne at his expense, over playing the role of modesty whilst nonchalantly letting it be known that no one can train horses as miraculously as he ... then thinks I, "That man has a horse to sell."' *Anon*

HEARTY GAMES

Advice to country children on how to conduct a snowball fight, from Cassell's *Book of Sports and Pastimes*, 1896:

'It is generally taken for granted that anyone has a perfect right to throw a snowball at anybody; this, however, is too sweeping an assumption, unless indulged in with a considerable amount of discretion, especially outside the playground, as boys have been known to get severe reprimands from policemen when the said boys have successfully thrown a snowball at some unoffending passer-by. Nevertheless, a good hearty game of snowballing, in a playground or other enclosed space, among a lot of lads divided into sides, produces much fun and excitement, and if spite be not introduced, is quite harmless. Let the youngsters take up their positions at the back, and busily occupy

themselves in the making of good, round and hard-pressed balls for their seniors standing in front, and so shielding them, to throw at the opposing force, and it will be astonishing to see how fast and furious the sport will proceed, imparting a rich glow of warmth and satisfaction to all the parties engaged.'

• If snowballing is a bit tame, the kids can try another outdoor game recommended by Cassells called Sling The Monkey. It sounds utterly horrendous: 'This is a game affording capital fun for all those whose lot it may be not to play the part of the monkey. Lots are to be drawn for the first monkey, who is suspended by the waist to one of the lower branches of a tree, so as just to be able to touch the ground with his toes. The players then being armed with that favourite schoolboy weapon, a knotted pocket handkerchief, and the monkey with a piece of chalk, it is the business of the player to whack the monkey, and of the monkey to chalk mark one or other of his tormentors. The tormentor who first receives a chalk-mark takes monkey's place. Any player hitting the monkey for the time being on the head or above the shoulders has also to be punished by being made to take monkey's place.' Capital fun indeed.

• The late, great gentleman writer Douglas Sutherland disapproved of upper-class country children being forced into playing outdoor games against their will: 'The most serious misdemeanour of which a child can be guilty in the eyes of his

parents is to sit around doing nothing. Doing nothing includes such things as collapsing exhausted in an arm chair after a particularly strenuous game, or even worse, curling up with a good book. "Oh do take your nose out of that beastly book. You will ruin your eyes. Why don't you go out and play in the nice warm rain?" Games are constantly being organized. Tennis tournaments are arranged with beastly cousins and neighbouring children, French cricket, rounders, croquet, prisoner's base, treasure hunts, and so on, which would be impossible for lucky children in small houses with neat gardens. Almost all Gentlemen's Children are brought up in country houses surrounded by simply acres and acres of jungle and mossy lawns.'

From The English Gentleman's Child, *published by Debrett, 1979*

INELEGANCIES

'Never appear in public on horseback unless you have mastered the inelegancies attending a first appearance in the saddle.'

From Decorum: A Practical Treatise on Etiquette, *J.A. Ruth & Co., 1877*

THE PROGRESS OF A RUSTIC BEAUTY

Victorian novelist Mary Russell Mitford offers her views on the village girl:

'The first appearance of the little lass is something after the manner of a caterpillar, crawling and creeping upon the grass, set down to roll by some tired little nurse of an eldest sister, or mother with her hands full. There it lies – a fat, boneless, rosy piece of health, aspiring to the accomplishment of walking and talking; stretching out its chubby limbs; scrambling and sprawling; laughing and roaring; there it sits, in all the dignity of the baby, adorned in a pink-checked frock, a blue spotted pinafore, and a little white cap, tolerably clean, and quite whole. One is forced to ask if it be boy or girl; for these hardy country rogues are all alike, open-eyed, and weather-stained, and nothing fearing. There is no more mark of sex in the countenance than in the dress.

'In the next stage, dirt-encrusted enough to pass for the chrysalis, if it were not so very unquiet, the gender remains equally uncertain. It is a fine, stout, curly-pated creature of three or four, playing and rolling about, amongst grass or mud, all day long; shouting, jumping, screeching – the happiest compound of noise and idleness, rags and rebellion, that ever trod the earth.

'Then comes a sunburnt gipsy of six, beginning to grow tall and thin, and to find the cares of the world gathering about her; with a pitcher in one hand, a mop in the other, an old straw bonnet of ambiguous shape, half hiding her tangled hair; a tattered stuff petticoat, once green, hanging below an equally tattered cotton frock, once purple; her longing eyes fixed on a game of base-ball at the corner of the green, till she reaches the cottage door, flings down the mop and pitcher, and darts off to her companions, quite regardless of the storm of scolding with which the mother follows her runaway steps.

'At ten, the little damsel gets admission to the charity school, and trips mincingly thither every morning, dressed in the old-fashioned blue gown, and white cap, and tippet, and bib and apron of that primitive institution, looking as demure as a nun, and as tidy; her thoughts fixed on button-holes, and spelling-books, those ensigns of promotion; despising dirt and base-ball, and all their joys.

'Then at twelve, the little lass comes home again, uncapped, untippeted, unschooled; brown as a berry, wild as a colt, busy as a bee – working in the fields, digging in the garden, frying rashers, boiling potatoes, shelling beans, darning stockings, nursing children, feeding pigs – all these employments varied by occasional fits of romping, and flirting, and idle play, according as the nascent coquetry, or the lurking love of sport, happens to preponderate; merry, and pretty, and good with all her little faults. It would be well if a country girl could stand at thirteen. Then she is charming. But the clock will move forward, and at fourteen she gets a service in a neighbouring town; and her next appearance is in the perfection of the butterfly state, fluttering, glittering, inconstant, vain – the gayest and gaudiest insect that ever skimmed over a village green. And this is the true progress of a rustic beauty, the average lot of our country girls; so they spring up, flourish, change and disappear.

Some indeed marry and fix amongst us, and then ensues another set of changes, rather more gradual, perhaps, but quite as sure, till grey hairs, wrinkles, and linsey-woolsey, wind up the picture.'

Miss Mitford had more time for country lads: 'If woman be a mutable creature, man is not … There is very little change in them from early boyhood. "The child is father to the man" in more senses than one. There is a constancy about them; they keep the same faces, however ugly; the same habits, however strange; the same fashions, however unfashionable; they are in nothing new-fangled.'

BEE AND WASP FACTS ...

BEES

Honey bees are the only insects that produce food for humans (as distinct from certain insects that *are* food for humans).

A single hive contains approximately 40,000–45,000 bees. Honey is the only food that includes all the substances necessary to sustain life, including enzymes, vitamins, minerals, and water. It is the only food that contains pinocembrin, an antioxidant associated with brain functioning.

A honey bee travels an average of 1,600 round trips in order to produce one ounce of honey; up to six miles per trip. To produce two pounds of honey, bees travel a distance equal to four times around the earth and visit about four million flowers.

Bees fly at 13–15 mph. Their wings flap 11,000 times per minute.

The bee's brain is oval in shape and the size of a sesame seed.

Bumblebees will not die if they use their sting, whereas honey bees will.

The bumblebee sting is much worse than a honey bee's.

Apiarists say that you should never use bad language in front of bees or they will sting you. (So, if you've just been stung, it might compound the problem to say 'Oh ****, I've just been stung'.) Likewise they are more likely to attack if you are wearing dark clothes.

• Folklore dictates that you should tell your bees everything that is going on in your life or they will either fly away or die (of boredom?):

> Marriage, birth or buryin',
> News across the seas,
> All your sad or merryin'
> You must tell the bees.

WASPS

Wasps are most aggressive from August to October.

When the sun goes down, wasps become inactive. This is the best time to attack their nests.

Wasps are beneficial to farmers since they eat caterpillars which can damage crops.

Only female wasps sting. The stinger doubles as the female sex organ.

A wasp lives no more than twenty-two days.

Wasps make their nests from chewed and pulped wood, which is why wasp nests resemble cardboard.

A single wasp colony may contain 2,000 insects.

AND WHEN THEY STING YOU …

Wasp sting venom is alkaline, so its painful effects are neutralised with vinegar. Bee sting venom is acidic and so its effects are reduced with an alkali such as bicarbonate of soda. Both bee and wasp venom contain other ingredients so the above remedies may not kill the pain completely. Try oral antihistamines and calamine lotion.

Traditional bee sting remedies include covering the affected area with tobacco paste (the contents of a cigarette mashed with a teaspoon of water), salt, baking soda, meat tenderiser, sliced onion, plantain leaves, toothpaste, clay, garlic, onions, charcoal, aspirin, apple cider vinegar (even though these two substances are acidic), mud, and even urine. Some people swear by taping a copper penny over the sting and leaving it there for fifteen minutes. An old pre-decimal penny is best because the copper content is higher.

• Nineteenth-century American bee expert Lorenzo Lorraine Langstroth described a 'highly amusing' bee sting remedy in his 1857 book *A Practical Treatise on the Hive and Honey-Bee*. It must be said that the following wheeze might not be everybody's idea of 'highly amusing': 'An old English Apiarian says … let the person who has been stung, catch as speedily as possible, another bee, and make it sting on the same spot. It requires some courage to venture upon such a singular homeopathic remedy; but as this old writer had previously stated, what I had verified in my own experience, that the oftener a person was stung, the less he suffered from the venom, I determined to make trial of his prescription. Allowing a sting to remain until it had discharged all its venom, I compelled another bee to insert its sting, as near as possible, in the same spot. I used no remedies of any kind, and had the satisfaction, in my zeal for new discoveries, of suffering more from the pain and swelling, than I had previously done for years.'

• Statistically, an American is more likely to die from a bee sting than a terrorist attack.

• There is a positive side to a bee sting. A correspondent to the 1871 Journal of Horticulture, noted that 'a bee sting or two in hot, sultry weather benefits gardeners by causing them to perspire more freely, and feel much lighter afterwards'.

GOOD

'Anybody can be good in the country.'

Oscar Wilde, The Picture of Dorian Gray, *1890*

BRUSH AND DOUBLE BRUSH

BRITAIN'S MOST FAMOUS HEDGELAYER is the Prince of Wales, who spends hours pottering along the hedgerows at his Gloucestershire estate Highgrove creating such works of art as 'Midland Bullocks' and 'Welsh Borders'.

Dressed in sturdy work boots and flat cap, Charles has laid hundreds of yards of hedge since learning the skill in the late 1990s. He has hosted the National Hedgelaying Championships at Highgrove and is the much-loved patron of the National Hedgelaying Society, a stupendously archaic organisation dedicated to the conservation of Britain's hedgerows through traditional skills.

Laying hedges is just one way of managing hedgerows. The society explains: 'Other techniques include "trimming" and "coppicing" (cutting off at ground level to encourage the hedge to regenerate). Left unmanaged a hedgerow will continue to grow upwards and outwards and will eventually become a line of trees. Where farmers keep cattle or sheep a good hedge is essential, for although barbed wire fences can easily be erected they do not provide shelter like a hedge. Hedges are also important for our wildlife and for their scenic value.'

Different hedges found throughout Britain include:

The Midland bullock: tough as hell and designed to stop cattle knocking them down. Finished height of 4 feet 6 inches. Hazel binders are woven along the top to give maximum strength. One side is stem and the other bushy growth. Livestock would be on the brush side with an arable field on the other side.

The Welsh Border: a double brush hedge with stakes driven in at a 35-degree slant. Dead wood is used to protect the re-growth from being browsed by stock.

The Derbyshire: again the brush is on the livestock side. Sawn timber stakes are used instead of hazel and are driven in on the brush side 30–36 inches apart. The hedge is trimmed to give a finished height of 4 feet. The base of the hedge is dug over to remove intrusive weeds. Bottom growth is encouraged in order to restrain sheep.

The South of England: this hedge is cut and laid over to create a double brush. A single line of stakes is placed at 18-inch intervals in the centre, with the top bound. Both sides of the hedge are trimmed.

The Lancashire and Westmorland: a hedge to keep out both cattle and sheep. Stakes are placed 18 inches apart on alternate sides with the stems laid between at 45 degrees. The stems are woven around the stakes and the hedge finished to a height of at least 3 feet 6 inches. The hedge is square cut.

The Yorkshire: for where a field is used for arable/sheep rotation. A very thin hedge on the basis that it will hold no stock for up to five years. This gives the laid hedge time to regenerate. The hedge is cut close to the ground with plenty of thickness of material in the bottom. Sawn stakes and rails are used to finish it off.

The Devon: this hedge is normally laid on top of a bank, which forms the main barrier against livestock. Densely packed brush is used to keep sheep and lambs secure.

The North Somerset: a row of stakes placed alternately on either side of the hedge holds the stems in place.

> • Under the Hedgerows Regulations 1997 it is against the law to remove or destroy hedges that are more than twenty metres long and more than thirty years old.

> • Government rural watchdog Natural England says you should avoid trimming hedgerows between the bird nesting season of 1st March to 31st July. Trimming a hedge too severely can be detrimental to bird life. Rather annoyingly but true to form, Natural England add that 'livestock should be fenced away from hedgerows, and a strip of uncultivated or ungrazed land maintained between the hedge and the adjacent crop'. Which surely destroys the whole point of a hedge in the first place!

STRAIGHT BOSOMS

The Archers, BBC Radio 4's everyday story of country folk, is Britain's longest-running soap opera. It started on 29th May, 1950, as a regional programme in the Midlands. The following year it went national and now boasts over five million listeners. Since the axing of the American soap opera *Guiding Light* in September 2009, *The Archers* is also the world's longest-running soap.

The following are some *Archers* quotes:

Lynda, discussing Ambridge Christmas panto music with Fallon: 'I had considered asking Valda but, strictly between you and me, she doesn't thrive in the pressure cooker of pantomime.'

Nigel: 'Are my bosoms straight?'
David: 'They are spectacular.'

Eddie: 'Are you doing the whole basket of ironing now?'
Clarrie: 'No, the queen of the fairies is taking over in five minutes.'

Nigel: 'Tally ho!' (After jumping into what he thought was Shula's bed but which turned out to be her father's.)

• Such was the outpouring of emotion in November 2006, following the cliff-hanger story line involving the love triangle between David, Ruth and herdsman Sam Batton, that there were 1.2 million page hits on the series' website. (Ruth finally concluded that shagging Sam was out of the question.)

• The theme of the working-class Grundy family being stomped upon by the middle-class Archers led Labour's Neil 'Welsh Windbag' Kinnock to call for the programme to be re-titled 'The Grundys and their Oppressors'.

• An organisation called @rchers @narchists insists that the Archers are real people: '*The Archers* is a real life fly-on-the-wall documentary about one of the strangest villages in England', proclaims the @@ website. 'Ambridge is a village inhabited by social misfits, murderers and nauseatingly cosy people. The most mild-mannered listeners would like to pour boiling oil on the likes of Shulugh, Rooooth, Dave and Loathsome Lizzie. It is a village so smug that even the animals are irritating.'

• Hundreds of listeners complained to the BBC after *Archers* posh bloke Nigel Pargetter fell to his death from a roof as part of a blockbuster sixtieth anniversary storyline. His last 'words' were a bloodcurdling scream and his demise prompted numerous internet spoofs, many ending with a loud, theatrical 'splat'. In one alternative ending Nige announces, 'What jolly luck – I've landed on the trampoline!'

• An utterly meaningless list of dogs featured throughout the ages in *The Archers*:
Bettina: Afghan hound owned by Mrs Antrobus.
Captain: Jack Woolley's Staffordshire bull terrier; fathered nine puppies by an Afghan hound called Portia, but how did he reach?
Charlie: Nelson's cocker spaniel bitch.

Charles Peregrine III: Old English sheepdog, owned by Caroline. Crap sheepdog – shot for worrying sheep.

Gyp: Jethro's dog bought for him by Phil Archer; died in a fire at Grange Farm, 1996.

Hermes: The runt of Captain and Portia's pups.

Jet: mutt rescued by David Archer.

JR: Robin Stokes's Jack Russell.

Leo: Great Dane owned by Caroline Bone.

Meg: William Grundy's border collie.

Mitch: owned by Greg Turner, who trained him to growl whenever he heard the name Matt Crawford.

Nell: Dan's sheepdog .

Patch: Robin Stokes's Old English sheepdog; died after eating a poisoned egg that was meant to kill crows.

Portia: Another of Mrs Antrobus's Afghans.

Scruff: German shepherd acquired by Shula and Alistair in August 2003 as the anti horse-slasher guard dog.

Tess: Grundy family pet; uncertain parentage.

Winston: Vile terrier stray found injured by Rosemary Tarrant in 1989; put down after a series of attacks.

Information courtesy of The Archers Addicts *website*: www.thearchers.co.uk

• Eight ferrets owned by Eddie Grundy: Grant, Mr Archer, Mrs Archer, Mr Noah, Mrs Noah, Peggy, Phil and Tex.

• Only one hamster has appeared in *The Archers* – Harry the Hamster, given to Daniel Lloyd by his adoptive father, Alistair.

• *The Archers'* worst-behaved animal was a pig, called Eric with a fondness for trashing gardens.

• *The Archers'* production team proved they understood little about country sports in 2011 when bad boy Matt Crawford was taken pheasant shooting despite being recently released from a prison sentence. Shoot expert Graham Downing of The Countryside Alliance pointed out that under Section 21 of the Firearms Act (1968) a person who has served a term of imprisonment in excess of three months is prohibited from possessing shotguns for five years from the date of his release. Matt should not have been shooting and his host Brian Aldridge should not have lent him a gun.

FREE FROM TUMULT

How sacred and how innocent
A country-life appears,
How free from tumult, discontent,
From flattery or fears!

From 'A Country Life',
by Anglo-Welsh bard Katherine Philips, 1632–1664:
Ms Philips was Britain's first lesbian poet

ESSENCE OF STOMACH ACHE

SOME FACTS about that sworn enemy of prep school boys, the dreaded rhubarb:

Rhubarb is native to Asia and grows wild in Siberia. Hardy and frost-resistant, it is a relative of buckwheat.

The Chinese first cultivated rhubarb in 2700 BC. The word rhubarb comes from the Latin *rhabarbarum* meaning 'root of the barbarians' because the Romans believed people who ate it to be barbaric in nature.

The plant became popular in seventeenth-century England with the availability of cheap sugar to sweeten it.

Rhubarb is a laxative.

Rhubarb leaves contain a toxin called oxalate – eleven pounds would kill a human. The juice of boiled-up leaves can be used as an insecticide.

Rhubarb is good for the liver. In the Middle Ages rhubarb was ground into powder and used medicinally as protection against scurvy. By the mid-seventeenth century rhubarb was double the price of opium in England.

Because rhubarb contains high concentrations of oxalates, it is bad for gout or bone problems such as osteoporosis.

The nineteenth-century American satirist Ambrose Bierce hated rhubarb so much that he described it as 'the essence of stomach ache'.

The redder the stalk, the sweeter the taste.

Only two garden vegetables are perennial and can keep producing for several growing seasons – asparagus and rhubarb.

To clean a burned cooking pot, rub a rhubarb stick on it.

• 'The Rhubarb Tart Song', written by comedian John Cleese for *The 1948 Show*, includes the unforgettable lines:

'Read all the existentialist philosophers, Like Schopenhauer and Jean-Paul Sartre. Even Martin Heidegger agrees on one thing: Eternal happiness is rhubarb tart.'

• The 'Rhubarb Triangle' is an area in Yorkshire, encompassing Wakefield, Leeds and Morley, which is famous for producing huge amounts of early forced rhubarb. In the early 1800s the fields were fertilised with human excrement from the nearby cities. These days Yorkshire rhubarb growers still encourage their crops with woollen waste rich in nitrogen known as 'shoddy'. The rhubarb plants spend two years in the fields before being transferred to heated sheds, where they are grown in darkness. Forced, shed-produced rhubarb is tenderer than that grown outdoors.

ISSUES

'I am not involved in any "issues" because it's too sensitive for me – or my wife – to get involved. Every time we express an opinion it becomes a whole thing in itself. And the whole purpose of living in the countryside was to get away from hundreds of people. My wife fell off a horse, and suddenly there are hundreds of people around.'

Film-maker Guy Ritchie, who moved with his then wife, the singer Madonna, to a country estate in Wiltshire

The 'issues' Ritchie referred to were country sports – he is a keen shot. Madonna took up shooting and thought about going hunting until she came over all vegan, split up from Ritchie, and changed her image yet again.

MORRISH DANCERS

John Worlidge was a seventeenth-century Hampshire squire who wrote on everything from farming to viniculture. In his 1676 work *Vinetum Britannicum: A Treatise of Cider*, Worlidge argued that Britain's climate and resources made the country ideal for producing cider rather than wine. Worlidge declared that cider was the answer to a long life. To prove his point he cited the case of eight Herefordshire morris dancers whose combined ages added up to 800 years – the youngest, Mr Pidgeon, was 79 and the eldest, Mr Corley, 109. Apparently the old boys put on a fine display.

Worlidge declared: 'They were constant cider drinkers. The daily use of cider either simple or diluted, hath been found by long experience to avail much to health and long life, preserving the drinkers of it in their full strength and vigour even to very old age.'

> • John Worlidge hated thieves who roamed the countryside with a passion. In a seventeenth-century world blessedly free of pinko liberalism, Worlidge was able to recommend some tough remedies. He declared that, in order to catch your thief, you needed to lay a variety of gin traps to 'keep him by the legs' until you released him. Invisible cheese wire strung across a door and sharp spikes embedded in the ground were a topping idea: 'By stumbling at the wire, the thief falls onto the spikes.'

CONSERVATIVE VALUES

COUNTRY PEOPLE believe their communities should be the preserve of white middle-class families with conservative values, according to a survey by Leicester University academics, who interviewed hundreds of village residents from across rural England:

'The countryside was, for a number of those we spoke to, the last bastion of old-fashioned Englishness which needed to be preserved from the encroachment of the "evils of modernity",' explained researcher Jon Garland. 'English country life is essentially monocultural, in all its forms – white, heterosexual, middle-class, conformist, family-orientated, church-going, conservative and "safe".'

Unsurprisingly, incomers to villages from ethnic minorities were treated with suspicion: 'The presence of a minority ethnic family suggested that the city was somehow invading the space of the tranquil rural the villagers so treasured. For many people, notions of Englishness are very much bound up with images of an unspoilt countryside and its gently undulating landscape of farms, cottages and hedgerows, itself a very nostalgic form of national identity redolent of an England left behind many decades ago.'

• The producer of ITV crime drama *Midsomer Murders* created a storm in 2011 when he admitted keeping ethnic minority characters out of the show's storylines because 'it wouldn't be an English village if there was any racial diversity'. The show's fans generally agreed with him.

QUIETEST

The quietest place in Britain is the quadrangle of St John's College, Oxford, where noise levels have been measured at below 50 decibels, no noisier than the hum of a refrigerator. The quietest town in Britain is Torquay, the Devon retirement backwater, which comes in at just 60.2 decibels, the same as a normal conversation. Britain's noisiest city is Newcastle – 80.4 decibels – where experts say that the incessant roar of traffic can seriously damage your health. Being in Newcastle's rush hour is the equivalent of having an alarm clock strapped to your ear.

POVERTY

THE AVERAGE WEEKLY FOOD BUDGET IN 1913 for a farm labourer, his wife, and four young children (approximate 2012 values in brackets):

> Bread, 21 loaves: 5s 3d (£22.04)
> Tea and cocoa: 1s 1½d (£4.75)
> Butter, 1lb, or margarine, 2lb: 1s (£4.20)
> Cheese, 4lb: 2s 8d (£11.19)
> Sugar, 4lb: 8d (£2.80)
> Bacon, meat, and suet: 3s 6d (£14.69)
> Oddments – salt, pepper, matches, etc: 1½d (£0.45)
> Flour: 9d (£3.15)
> Currants: 4d (£1.40)
> Treacle or jam: 4d (£1.40)
>
> Total weekly cost: 15s 9d (£66.07).

This total was roughly the man's weekly wage, leaving little money for anything else. The pre-First World War farm worker lived on the verge of poverty. Only by growing his own vegetables and scrounging milk and tiny amounts of meat from the farm was he able to get by. The average wage of an agricultural labourer in 2012 was around £350 per week. Hours worked nowadays would be around forty-five per week, considerably less than the farm worker of 1913, who toiled for ten hours a day, six days a week.

MOLE FACTS ...

As of 2011 there were an estimated 40 million moles in Britain. Since the 2006 ban on the use of strychnine, their numbers have increased dramatically.

Celebrity 'Mole Catcher of the Year', Ian Dando from Gloucestershire, catches around 8,000 moles annually. He prefers old-fashioned trapping.

The male mole grows up to seven inches in length and weighs up to four and a half ounces.

A mole can deploy a force equivalent to thirty-two times its bodyweight, giving it incredible digging ability – like a human being having JCB buckets attached to his arms.

A mole consumes fifty pounds of worms and insects each year.

Mole tunnels have different layers: near the surface are feed and travelling tunnels; living quarters are lower down.

Moles can dig surface tunnels at approximately eighteen feet per hour and can travel through existing tunnels at about eighty feet per minute.

Moles contain twice as much blood as mammals of similar size, enabling them to breathe underground with minimal amounts of oxygen.

Moles dislike the scent of human beings.

Moles cause havoc in churchyards, tunnelling under gravestones and making them tilt.

HOW TO GET RID OF 'EM:

Trapping is the most effective method of mole control. Traps should be set in active surface burrows. Since moles possess a highly developed sense of smell you should wear gloves while handling traps so your quarry is not put off by human scent.

If trapping fails, try pouring ammonium sulphate dissolved in warm water down the mole hole. Dettol and wood preservative are said to work as well, though professional mole-catchers dispute this. (Note: pouring diesel down the mole runs and setting fire to it does not work and will make your lawn look like Vietnam after a Tet Offensive.)

People have tried all sorts of other repellents: ground vibrators, sonic devices, chewing gum, broken glass. All are unproven.

Sitting in a deckchair watching over your lawn with a shotgun is unlikely to achieve much.

• Eighteenth-century Scottish poet and novelist James Hogg, known as the Ettrick Shepherd, was a great champion of the mole, which he described as 'an innocent and blessed little pioneer, who enriches our pastures annually with the first top-dressing, dug with great pains and labour from the fattest of the soil beneath'. Hogg was amazed that farmers wanted to exterminate moles: 'If a hundred men and horses were employed on a pasture farm of two thousand acres, in raising and driving manure for a top-dressing of that farm, they would not do it so effectually, so neatly, or so equally as the natural number of moles.'

BETTER AGAINST A WALL

LADY HILLINGDON, wife of Tory politician George, 2nd Baron Hillingdon, is the lady who confided that, when visited at night by her husband she would 'lie back and think of England'. She subsequently had a rose – apricot with purple leaves – named after her. This gave rise to the old gardening joke that the flower was good in a bed but much better up against a wall.

Lady H's full diary entry of 1912 read: 'I am happy now that George calls on my bedchamber less frequently than of old. As it is, I now endure but two calls a week, and when I hear his steps outside my door I lie down on my bed, close my eyes, open my legs and think of England'. The couple had three children.

FARMING CLOWNS

B ritain's most acerbic agricultural writer was Arthur Young (1741–1820) whose publication *Annals of Agriculture* became essential reading for landowners.

Clergyman's son Young started his career as a farm manager in Essex. He switched to writing and spent much of his life travelling through England, Wales, Ireland and France, reporting on changes in agriculture.

Young campaigned ceaselessly for agricultural reform. In the early 1780s he issued surveys to Britain's landowners asking them to report back on anything that would help the future of farming.

But the gentry could barely be bothered to respond to Young's tedious surveys. He received completed surveys from only ten of England's fifty-two counties. Nobody from Scotland or Ireland bothered to reply at all. Young was furious, blaming the gentry's preoccupation with hunting and the like. He exploded, 'Great exertions have been made on my part in procuring the most respectable correspondence and these are the thanks I receive!'

Young despised gentleman farmers reluctant to share the results of their agricultural experiments. Such 'clowns' made him angry. In a biting polemic, he snarled, 'Did they receive an education from their parents, in order to eat, drink, steep, live, die, and rot in oblivion? The horse in their stable can do all this.'

• In 1793 Arthur Young became the first secretary to the British government's newly created Board of Agriculture, established as a response to the war with France which was threatening Britain's food supplies.

• *Annals of Agriculture* attracted big-name contributors such as King George III, who, writing under the pseudonym of 'Ralph Robinson of Windsor', submitted lengthy and fairly boring tracts on the minutiae of ploughing and the like.

GIGANTIC JAPANESE 4X4

In 2001 the Left-wing publication *New Statesman* lambasted the new breed of countryman taking over Britain's most beautiful villages. The magazine savaged management consultants like 'Nigel, wearing brass-buttoned blazers and with a gigantic Japanese 4x4 parked up on the Olde Smithy's gravel drive'.

Nigel was joined by 'myriad clones' like Nicholas, who was big in publishing; Henry, a cocoa trader, and Jason, a reality TV producer: 'They are the new squires of Dungpong-cum-Blasterheath and countless village communities going westward-ho to Cornwall and north to the Dales. They are the proud spear-carriers of the most dramatic reversal of human migration in Britain since the Industrial Revolution, when poverty drove ploughmen and milkmaids into the cotton mills of Lancashire and the iron foundries and coal mines of South Wales.'

Author Peter Dunn added: 'The essential difference with the tidal wave of 21st-century urban migrants (50,000 a year from London alone) is that most of them are rich beyond the dreams of an older generation of country folk, who can no longer afford to buy their ancestors' village homes.'

THE DEVIL'S OWN JOB

ADVICE ON SPINNING WOOL by 1930s Scottish crofting writer Margaret Mary Leigh:

'To the beginner, spinning is the devil's own job. It takes about a fortnight to learn to spin with competence. Like many other things it cannot be taught; you must just practise till you get the knack, and try to master your temper. The wheel must be controlled with your feet and the yarn with your hands; the problem is to work them together, and the worst moment is the joining of one carded roll to another without stopping the wheel or allowing the yarn end to run out of your hand and on to the bobbin – a thing it will do every other minute; and this means tedious re-threading with a bent hairpin, and fury and despair. Or the wheel will suddenly run in reverse, with tangle and confusion. … If the wool goes on to the bobbin too quickly, it will be thick and lumpy; if too slowly, it will over twist and break.'

HEAT PRICKLY

A recipe for Hedgehog Carbonara (serves four):

> 500g spaghetti
> 30ml olive oil
> 250g lean hedgehog
> 1 medium onion (chopped)
> 125ml water
> 60ml dry white wine
> 4 eggs
> 60ml double cream
> 100g grated parmesan cheese

Chop hedgehog into small chunks. Beat eggs and cream together in a bowl. Add half the parmesan cheese. Put onions and hedgehog chunks in pan with olive oil on medium heat until onions are almost clear. Add wine and reduce heat. Combine cooked pasta with egg, cream and cheese mix. Add hedgehog, onions and wine and mix thoroughly. Garnish with parmesan. Lie to the children and says it's chicken …

Note: use road kill: you should not kill hedgehogs intentionally.

WATER KILLERS

The Environment Agency's 10 worst alien invaders of Britain's waterways:

1. Killer shrimp
2. Water primrose
3. Floating pennywort
4. American signal crayfish
5. Topmouth gudgeon
6. Giant hogweed
7. Japanese knotweed
8. Himalayan balsam
9. Mink
10. Parrot's feather

COMPLETELY CUCKOO

The first 'first cuckoo' letters to *The Times* appeared in the 1850s and proliferated thereafter. Correspondence included a missive from a Mr Raymond Thrupp who, on 10th April, 1886, considered it important enough to alert the world to the fact that the previous Sunday he had heard the bird twice in Richmond Park. And on 1st April, 1890, Mr W.J. Stevenson recorded that the cuckoo had been heard near Surbiton railway station by a relative of his 'who is a resident in this highly-favoured spot'.

• Long before *The Times'* cuckoo correspondence, publications such as the *Farmer's Gazette* always noted each year when the bird's call was first heard.

• A correspondent calling himself 'A Hedge Sparrow' wrote a spoof letter to *The Times* in 1864 saying that the cuckoo had been heard by four people close to his village as early as 16th March. The letter was headlined 'Stupid as a Cuckoo'.

• There was a custom in Shropshire during the 1820s whereby the moment the first cuckoo was heard farm workers would down tools and devote the rest of the day to 'mirth and jollity', i.e. getting hog-whimpered on what was known as 'cuckoo ale'.

• Folklore has it that the cuckoo sings from St Tiburtius's Day (14th April) to St John's Day (24th June). Superstition decrees that if you hear the cuckoo sing on St Tiburtius's Day, you should turn over all the money in your pockets, spit and not look at the ground.

SWIMMING IN STREAMS

Cheer'd by the milder beam, the sprightly youth
Speeds to the well known pool, whose crystal depth
A sandy bottom shows. A while he stands
Gazing th' inverted landscape, half afraid
To meditate the blue profound below;
Then plunges headlong down the circling flood.

From 'The Four Seasons: Summer' by Scottish poet James Thomson (1700–1748)

• 'The best times for swimming are before breakfast, or between the hours of seven and eight in the morning, during the months of May, June, July, and August, and part of September, but it may also be practised in the middle of the day ... The sea is the best place for swimming in; running rivers, and the 'brook that brawls along' are next to be chosen; and the still, dull pond, the last. In either case, the bottom ought to be of gravel, or smooth stones, but quite free from holes, so that there may be no danger of hurting the feet, or sinking in the mud. Weeds must be carefully avoided, lest the feet get entangled amongst them. The swimmer should ascertain that the bottom of the stream be not beyond his depth; and if he has no one with him who is acquainted with the spot, he should endeavour to fathom it before venturing in. Bathing is best performed when entirely naked: but, if this be unsuitable, short drawers may be worn.'

Samuel Williams, The Boy's Treasury of Sports, Pastimes and Recreations, *1844*

• 'When I was a boy, I amused myself one day with flying a paper kite; and approaching the banks of a lake which was near a mile broad, I tied the string to a stake, and the kite ascended to a very considerable height above the pond, while I was swimming. In a little time, being desirous of amusing myself with my kite, and enjoying at the same time the pleasure of swimming, I returned, and loosing from the stake the string with the little stick which was fastened to it, went again into the water, where I found that, lying on my back, and holding the stick in my hand, I was drawn along the surface of the water in a very agreeable manner. ... I have never since that time practised this singular mode of swimming, though I think it not impossible to cross, in this manner, from Dover to Calais. The packet-boat, however, is still preferable.'

*Dr Benjamin Franklin (1706–1790)
Founding Father of the United States
and fanatical swimmer*

RURAL GRAFFITI

'Not a Beech but bears some cipher,
Tender word, or amorous text.'

Eighteenth-century poet James Thomson

Argument rages about whether you should carve your initials – perhaps with your lover's name dreamily intertwined with a heart – onto a tree. But if you want to leave your mark this way it's best to use a beech: the bark is smooth and you will not damage a mature tree if you cut lightly with a sharp pocket knife. The cut will heal, leaving a scab. But be warned: ecobores will disapprove, ludicrously claiming that the tree will silently howl with pain when you cut it, so it's best to keep your carving to yourself.

• Tree carvings are known as arborglyphs; most famous arborglyphite was Helen of Troy, who carved her lover's name on a beech.

• Scottish poet Thomas Campbell (1777–1844) wrote 'The Beech Tree's Petition' in which a beech tree asks the woodman not to cut it down because of the many lovers' names inscribed on its trunk:

> Thrice twenty summers I have seen
> The sky grow bright, the forest green;
> And many a wintry wind have stood
> In bloomless, fruitless solitude,
> Since childhood in my pleasant bower
> First spent its sweet and sportive hour;
> Since youthful lovers in my shade
> Their vows of truth and rapture made,
> And on my trunk's surviving frame
> Carved many a long-forgotten name.
> Oh! by the sighs of gentle sound,
> First breathed upon this sacred ground;
> By all that Love has whispered here,
> Or Beauty heard with ravished ear;
> As Love's own altar honour me:
> Spare, woodman, spare the beechen tree!

STRONG BOXES

OF THE 28,000 PILL BOXES BUILT DURING 1940–41 as defences against an expected German invasion, around 6,000 remain littered across the countryside. The most common pill boxes are types 22 (regular hexagon) and 24 (irregular hexagon), type 24 being the most frequent.

Second World War pill boxes comprise a small room ten feet square and six feet high with rough concrete walls and small slits for machine guns. After the war farmers were offered £5 per pill box to knock them down, but such was the strength of their construction that demolition was often more trouble than it was worth. As a result, hundreds remain, particularly in the South West where a German landing was considered most likely. The most complete line of pill boxes – dubbed the Twentieth Century Hadrian's Wall – runs from Seaton, Devon to Bridgewater, Somerset. It consists of 280 pill boxes with machine gun emplacements every few hundred yards.

Despite their historical importance, alarmingly few of Britain's surviving Second World War defences have Listed Building protection.

MANGELLING SONGS

THE ONLY POP GROUP whose songs are dedicated to rural matters is The Wurzels, a West Country outfit that has brought us such ditties as 'The Combine Harvester' (Number One in the UK charts for two weeks in 1976, selling 400,000 copies; based on 'Brand New Key' by the singer Melanie) and 'I Am A Cider Drinker' (also 1976, a truly dreadful number based on Jonathan King's 'Una Paloma Blanca'). The Wurzels continue to perform regular gigs and are as popular as ever. 'The Combine Harvester' is still one of the most requested songs at hunt balls.

FLY TIP

EXPERT FISHERMEN say that if you wish to dye your panama hat to a neutral brown or green for use on the river you should use a wood dye as this also helps to repel insects.

SENSIBLE SHOES

B ROGUES, that most countrified style of footwear, are a modern development of the old rawhide boot favoured by Irish peasantry and Scottish Highlanders. They were made with hide punctured with holes to let water out. Brogues do not have the tongue which covers the bridge of the foot in normal shoes, thus allowing the shoe to dry quicker. The high lacing ensures that the shoe is not sucked off should it become stuck in mud.

• Full brogues are characterised by a pointed toe cap with extensions (wings) that run along both sides of the toe, terminating near the ball of the foot. The toe cap of a full brogue is both perforated and serrated along its edges and includes additional decorative perforations in the centre.

• Half-brogues feature a toe cap with decorative perforations and serration along the cap's edge and include additional decorative perforations in the centre of the toe cap. The half brogue was first produced in 1937 by London cobbler John Lobb, who wanted to offer his customers a shoe more casual than a plain Oxford yet more refined than a full brogue.

• Quarter-brogues have a toe cap with decorative perforations and serrations along the cap's edge. Unlike semi-brogues, quarter-brogues have no decorative perforations in the centre of the toe cap.

• American 'longwing' brogues feature a pointed toe cap with wings that extend the full length of the shoe, meeting at a centre seam at the heel. Worn during the 1970s by New York drug dealers (as seen in the film *Superfly*) they are utterly unacceptable in Britain and not really brogues at all.

• The word 'brogues' is a derivation of the Gaelic 'brög', taken from the Old Norse 'brók' meaning 'leg covering'.

• Brogues should never be worn with morning dress. Black plain toe-capped Oxfords only. Never wear full brogues to a funeral as they are considered too ornate for a solemn occasion. Half, or possibly quarter, brogues are acceptable. Always black, never brown.

• Highland dancers wear a lighter type of brogue known as 'dancing ghillies'.

RANDOM BLOBS

A random glossary of obscure farming terminology:

Baconer: a finished pig sold for bacon, older and larger than a porker.

Blob marker: a device that leaves a temporary trail of foam blobs so that a tractor driver can see where he has been working.

Clarts: mud (northern England and southern Scotland).

Dag: sheep wool clogged with dung, usually under the tail. If allowed to remain, dags may become infested with maggots, which can infest the flesh of the living sheep. Dagging is the unpleasant job of trimming the dags.

Dubs: mud (southern Scotland).

Flink: very odd word for twelve or more cattle in a group.

Gelt: an adult ewe that is not in lamb when others are, usually because of problems at a previous lambing.

Gimmer: a female sheep that has been weaned but not yet sheared; about six to fifteen months old.

Hagberg Falling Number: a measure of the quality of wheat.

Haulms: the stems of potato plants.

Hefting: the acclimatising of a flock of hill sheep to 'their' part of the hillside.

Lairage: a place where livestock are kept temporarily, commonly found at markets, ports and abattoirs.

Nurse crop: a shelter crop; a quick-growing, hardy crop sown thinly along with a tender, slower-growing crop in order to give shelter from harsh conditions during the early stages of growth. For example, winter sown oats, taken as silage in the spring, may be used to nurse field crops.

Poaching: damage caused to grassland when animals churn up the fields during wet weather. Known as 'stogging' in the West Country.

Rigwelted: a heavily pregnant ewe may roll over and be unable to right herself; she is rigwelted. (There is a brand of beer called Rigwelter which has a similar effect on humans.)

Septoria: a fungal disease of wheat, barley and oats.

Speaning: northern term for weaning, especially of lambs.

Yow: a slang term for a female sheep.

PISCIS AEGROTATIO

A splendid homily to fishing by author Colin McKelvie, from *A Country Naturalist's Year*, published by Swan Hill Press, 1993:

'If fishing is a disease, an addiction which is probably incurable and lifelong, if not directly life-threatening, then I can identify the precise moment of my infection. I was seven years old, I longed to catch a fish, and I came under the kindly tutelage of a retired Irish parson, who loved his fishing. He gave me my first rod, took me to catch my first trout – all of five ounces, from a hill loch – and fuelled some latent instinct to be a fly fisher. Even at that age, it was soon obvious to me that one trout could look very different from another. But why? How come that one little lake held tiny, blunt-headed fish with blood red spots while another, barely a mile away over the heather, was full of streamlined silvery trout with only a spangling of black speckles? And on the bigger waters, why did some trout I caught look so different from the others from the very same loch? I wanted to know more.

'Back at school, in the endless weeks of winter terms, the lochs of summer were a world away. But there were books about fish in the library. Some forgotten old boy had left his alma mater a wonderful collection of old books on wildlife and sport, and on grey afternoons when I'd managed to escape the muddy hooliganism of house rugby there were hours of delight, perching on the warmth of a massive cast-iron radiator and leafing through those books about fish by experts with imposing names like Gunther and Regan, Jardine and Grimble. From their pages tumbled a deluge of italicised Latin names of trout –

estuarius for the trout of river estuaries, *orcadensis* from the brackish lochs of Orkney, *gallivensis* for the sea trout of Connemara, *albus* and *brachypoma* for the sea trout of eastern English and Scottish coasts, but *cambricus* for their Welsh cousins. My Latin master might have coaxed a better O-level pass out of me if he had taught us about Latin fish names, instead of the conventional conjugations and declensions.'

TOP BUTTON HOLE

Top 5 best-selling cut flowers in the UK:

1. Carnation
2. Rose
3. Lily
4. Chrysanthemum
5. Daffodil

Survey by The Flowers and Plant Association

RURAL BRITAIN R.I.P.

1997–2008: Rural schools are closed down at the rate of one per month.

2008: 400 village shops closed.

2009: 900 country pubs closed.

1999–2009: 2,334 rural post offices closed.

2011: Rural bus services face massive cuts …

SUNK TO THE NECK

An 1856 publication called *Walker's Manly Exercises* offers this warning on the dangers of skating on the village pond:

'Skating on ice of doubtful strength is accompanied with great danger, as in an instant the skater may find himself sunk to the neck in water, and be drowned before assistance can be rendered. Much of this danger may be obviated by wearing a safety-cape, which is a loose cape inflated with air, the invention of a member of the Edinburgh skating club. … If the ice breaks and the skater finds that he cannot get away from rotten ice, he must crawl over it on his hands and knees, in order to reduce his weight on the supporting points. If he falls on it at length, he must roll away from it towards ice more firm. If he fall into a hole, he must extend his arms horizontally over the edges of the unbroken ice, and tread water till a ladder or plank is pushed towards him.'

SOW SLOW

OX-PLOUGHING ENDED IN BRITAIN IN 1929 when a farmer called Major Harding, from East Dean, Hampshire, disbanded his team of oxen. Over in Gloucestershire, Earl Bathurst retained six Herefords for ploughing but they were more of a tourist attraction than the genuine article.

Oxen can pull heavy loads much further than horses. Oxen are particularly good at ploughing in heavy clay. Working oxen usually require shoes – two for each hoof. Unlike horses, oxen find it tricky standing on three legs so shoeing is done by throwing the ox to the ground and lashing all four feet to a beam.

> If the farmer has no corn, no corn can he sow.
> Then the miller has no work for his mill also.
> And the baker has no bread for the poor to provide.
> If the plough should stand still we should all starve alive.

'The Ox-Plough Song', Trad. English

HARMONIOUS

THE SOUNDS OF THE ENGLISH COUNTRYSIDE changed forever with the decline of the English sheep bell. Until the Second World War the leader of a flock of sheep was distinguished with a bell around her neck, particularly where sheep were likely to get lost where pastures ran into woodland: hence the term 'bellwether' for the leader sheep. The old English sheep bell was a harmonious instrument with a deep sound, quite unlike the shrill continental variety heard in countries like Switzerland.

DOMESTIC TIP

In the old days the housekeeper in a country house would leave a broom
lying on the floor when a servant came for a job interview.
If the girl picked it up, she was hired on the spot.

WHY WE HATE RATS

Rats reach sexual maturity in eight weeks, have sex twenty times a day and
can give birth every month.

A single pair of rats can produce 2,000 offspring a year.

Rats eat anything, including rubbish.

Rats' teeth are harder than aluminium, allowing them to gnaw through cables.

Rats can swim up lavatory U-bends.

Rats can squeeze through a hole no larger than a man's thumb.

Rats damage 20 per cent of the world's crops.

Because of the diseases a rat carries, it is the only wild animal the SAS are
banned from eating in the field.

Mexicans eat rats.

There are more rats than humans on the planet – over six billion.

Rats urinate eighty times a day. Weil's disease is spread via their urine.

Contrary to popular belief, soda does not make rats explode.

• Following the demise of cock fighting, a new sport of rat hunting emerged in
Victorian London. One hundred rats would be put in a pit and a terrier dropped in
among them. Bets were taken on how long it would take the dog to kill the rats. The
record was held by an East London terrier called Billy, who could kill a hundred rats
in five minutes.

ONLY IN THE COUNTRY

'It is only in the country that we can get to know a person or a book.'

Cyril Connolly, The Unquiet Grave, *1945*

GOT ME A LINE

I'm going fishing
I got me a line
Nothin' I do's gonna' make the difference
So I'm taking the time
And you ain't never gonna be happy
Anyhow, anyway
So I'm going fishing
And I'm going today
I'm going fishing
Sounds crazy I know
I know nothing about fishing
But just watch me go.

The lyrics to 'Gone Fishing' by Chris Rea, from his 1991 album Auberge, *reprinted by kind permission of Warner/Chappell Music*

PREGNANT WITH GOUT

A recipe for jugged hare from an 1810 cook book called *Culina Fumulatrix Medicinae*, or *Receipts In Modern Cookery With A Medical Commentary*:

'Clean the hare and soak it in cold water for an hour. Then cut it into pieces and put them in a pan with a few peppercorns, a bundle of sweet herbs, one carrot, an onion stuck with cloves, and a little water. Stew gently over a low heat and in about two hours the gravy will be drawn from the meat. Strain and thicken the gravy with butter rolled in flour, adding some broth and a cupful of port. Season with white pepper, salt, and powdered mace. Give a gentle boil, and serve in a deep dish.'

The author, a doctor called A. Hunter, warns: 'This is a dish pregnant with gout, and should not be placed before a gouty gentleman who is not possessed of a large share of self-denial.'

A PICTURE OF SERENITY

One of the best pieces written in praise of coarse fishing, is Charles White's 1840 masterpiece, *Sporting Scenes and Country Characters*:

'A taste for angling, acquired in our boyish days, when we roam from stream to stream, is never forgotten. This tranquil art is, indeed, enjoyed by some of every class and of every age. On the river side may be observed the truant boy, just escaped from school, eagerly watching his trembling float and, not less interested in the sport, the humble artisan, provided with his tackle and his baits, leaves, for a time, the busy scene of his labours, and, desirous of

pursuing his favourite diversion in peace and quietness, as well as to enjoy the fresh air, to the benefits of which he is, perhaps, a stranger, trudges over the fields or through the green lanes, to some well-known haunt, where he knows that he has the best chance of having his exertions rewarded. Nor do those who move in a higher sphere, and possess similar tastes and feelings, despise the tranquil pursuit of float fishing. The float-fisher is generally the bearer of more rods than one; and while the heavier of the two is baited with a large dew-worm, and placed upon the bank, he angles with the other, casting an eye on both floats. The objects of his pursuit are numerous: the perch, the chub, the barbel, the bream, the roach, and the dace. In order to secure these, he uses various descriptions of baits, worms, gentles, creed-malt, wasp grubs, white bread, &c. The old hand despises all scented paste, and such matters; he generally prefers well-scoured brandling-worms, which will be taken by most descriptions of fish that are worth the wear and tear of tackle. This worm is a great favourite with one of the best and most nutritious classes of the finny-tribe, namely, the perch; and if the angler meet with a shoal of these, he will succeed in taking as many as he chooses, until they move off in another direction. The trout, bream, chub, and barbel, will also take this worm. Roach and dace afford pleasant, and not difficult angling. For killing these, the angler uses creed-malt; taking care, also, on the previous evening, to bait the place, by throwing a portion of grains into the stream, which has the effect of drawing them to the spot, for the purpose of feeding. Steadily watching the light float, he must strike upon the finest run, precisely in time, otherwise he loses his prize. The chub is taken, at the proper season, with, amongst other matters, the wasp-grub, which is a conspicuous bait. ... Many men of kind and gentle dispositions are float-fishers. The practice is suited to a peaceful and contemplative turn of mind; and thus, honest Izaak has called his work *The Contemplative Man's Recreation*. Pursuing his favourite amusement, he is delighted with the objects around him, in all their varied and attractive forms; and though, compared with the fly-fisher or the troller, his may be considered an inferior pursuit, yet the quietness and stillness in which he so much delights, and which are essential to his success, have charms for him which surpass all others. Seated beneath the wide-spread branches of the aged sycamore, he feels a mine of wealth in himself, of peace, contentment, and tranquillity. The bright beams of the sun dance or repose upon the pure river stream, and the shadow of his own green canopy forms a striking contrast on the water. He sees the small finny tribe disporting in the stream; he marks the laden barge move silently and sluggishly past; he hears the cheerful song of the lark on high; he traces the merry and ceaseless note of the sedge warbler close at hand; the lowing of the herds in the bright green pastures; the busy cry of the rooks in the neighbouring trees; the gaudy dragon-fly flickering over the stream; and the hum of the humble-bee as he goes hurrying homewards: in short, all sounds and sights which gladden his quiet retreat. Such are the contemplative pleasures of the musing angler, who is the picture of contentment, repose, and serenity.'

GAMP GUIDANCE

Rainy day note: if you must insist on carrying an umbrella in the countryside – the practice is considered by some as rather effete (why can't you wear a Barbour?) as well as being dangerous in lightning – it should be rolled and fastened, unless you are an Old Etonian, in which case it is accepted that an O.E. always carries his umbrella unfurled.

THATCHING FACTS

Statistically, the 60,000 thatched properties in Britain are no more likely to catch fire than those with a tile or slate roof. If you try to set fire to a closed, thick book, it will not burn easily owing to the compactness of the pages. The same is true of thatch.

There is an average of one thatch fire a week in Britain. Everything tends to go up. Insurers pay out an average £100,000 for a fire at a thatched property compared to £10,000 for the average house fire. Insurance premiums are roughly double what you would pay for a conventional property.

Ninety per cent of thatch fires relate to faulty chimneys and wood-burning stoves. Other fire risks include electrical faults, fireworks, garden bonfires, discarded cigarettes, and vermin – rats and mice can chew through wiring and cables, creating sparks.

Thatching was once the cheapest form of roofing. Now a lack of skilled thatchers has made it the most expensive.

Thatch keeps a house warm in winter and cool in summer.

Norfolk reed is the best thatch material, lasting up to sixty years. Combed wheat – also known as Devon reed – lasts up to forty years. Heather is still used in northern England and Scotland.

If you are buying a thatched property you must check its condition thoroughly. If fixings are exposed all over the roof, it indicates that the thatch is nearing the end of its life.

Once, most cottages in Britain were thatched. The decline of thatch began in the nineteenth century with the emergence of the railway network meaning that affordable Welsh slate could be delivered around the country. Also, the invention of the combine harvester meant that wheat straw was no longer usable for thatching.

In 1880, the parish church at Reyden, Suffolk, was roofed with straw at the back but tiles on the side facing the street because it was thought that modern tiles looked more elegant.

TOFF TOP

'A CLOTH CAP is assumed in folk mythology to represent working class, but it also denotes upper class affecting casualness. So it is undoubtedly classless, and there lies its strength. A toff can be a bit of a chap as well without, as it were, losing face.'

Former Daily Express *journalist Geoffrey Mather*

• The tweed cap, arguably the country gent's single most important item of clothing, can be traced back more than 500 years. In 1571, an Act of Parliament made it law that on Sundays and religious holidays all males over six years old, except for the educated and nobility, had to wear caps of wool manufactured in England or be fined three farthings a day. The idea was to stimulate the wool trade. The law lasted to the end of the sixteenth century but by then the cloth cap had become recognised as the mark of the working man. Every man and boy in England had one in his wardrobe. Around 1900 the tweed cap crossed from working class necessity to upper class fashion item. Tweed caps were the rage at Edwardian shooting parties and the Prince of Wales, later Edward VII, sported one in the Royal Family's tweed. Today, the only place for a gentleman to buy his tweed cap is Lock & Co. (founded 1676), in St James's, London, hatters to the Duke of Edinburgh and Prince Charles. You can buy cheap tweed caps at country stores around Britain but there always seems to be something unfortunately lumpy about them.

• The supermarket Asda has reported an increase in sales of tweed caps, particularly in the south of England. Displaying an unlikely knowledge of country sports, an Asda spokesman described their cap line as 'retro-shooting chic'.

• The trilby hat, the only headwear in which gentlemen should be seen at race meetings, was named after Trilby O'Ferrall, eponymous heroine of George du Maurier's 1894 novel. In the stage version of the book the character wore a soft, felt hat made from rabbit hair.

OLD JOKE

Two cows were chatting in the field:
''Ere', asks Daisy, 'Have you heard about this mad-cow disease?'
'Yeah, sounds nasty', replies Buttercup. 'Glad I'm a chicken.'

SWEET RATS

TO MAKE ROUGH CIDER you simply pulp the apples. They are best when they are old, yellow and wrinkly. No metal should be allowed to touch the fruit. Press out the juice, put into wooden barrels and leave to stand outside for six months. The best cider apples are Bramleys and Laxtons. Good cider should need nothing added to it, though you can try a taste 'improver' such as pig's blood, milk, diesel-soaked rags, dead sheep or the occasional dog. Down in Somerset (where cider is known as 'tanglefoot' because that's what it does to you), rats have traditionally been added.

Talking of rats in cider, the following cautionary tale was published in an 1870 American temperance pamphlet:

'A Farmer, in a flourishing town in Massachusetts, filled a hogshead with cider, leaving the bung-hole open so that the oxygen of the air might produce vinous fermentation … In the spring he was surprised to find that his cider was soft and sweet as unintoxicating wine. He and his family had all the cider they needed. In the fall, when he was about to cleanse the hogshead for a new supply of new cider, judge his astonishment when he made the discovery that half a bushel of bones, the skeletons of rats, was in the bottom of the hogshead. The flesh of the rats had been dissolved in the cider, and its sweetness was due to that fact.'

NOT FUNNY

'Villagers do not think that village cricket is funny.'

Cricket commentator John Arlott

ROBIN ROUND UP

THE ROBIN is one of the shortest-lived wild birds, with a life expectancy of five to six months; 60 per cent of all adult robins die each year.

Male robins are highly aggressive and will attack other males that stray into their territories. Such attacks account for up to 10 per cent of the deaths of adult robins, usually pecked to death through the base of the skull.

The robin first appeared on Christmas cards in the mid-nineteenth century. Anthony Trollope called postmen 'robins' because of their bright red waistcoats. Early cards depicted robins knocking at doors carrying envelopes in their beaks.

Cats avoid eating robins as the birds make them vomit.

• In the seventeenth century people believed that eating a robin (or, indeed a sparrow), would help break up kidney stones.

RURAL SHADE

> The statesman, lawyer, merchant, man of trade,
> Pants for the refuge of some rural shade,
> Where all his long anxieties forgot
> Amid the charms of a sequester'd spot,
> Or recollected only to gild o'er
> And add a smile to what was sweet before,
> He may possess the joys he thinks he sees,
> Lay his old age upon the lap of ease,
> Improve the remnant of his wasted span,
> And having liv'd a trifler, die a man.

'Retirement', by English poet William Cowper (1731–1800):
Cowper was one of the most popular poets of his day –
he wrote about anything to do with the
English countryside

MAGNIFICENCE

'Nothing can be more imposing than the magnificence of English park scenery. Vast lawns that extend like sheets of vivid green, with here and there clumps of gigantic trees, heaping up rich piles of foliage: the solemn pomp of groves and woodland glades, with the deer trooping in silent herds across them; the hare bounding away to the covert; or the pheasant, suddenly bursting upon the wing; the brook, taught to wind in natural meanderings, or expand into a glassy lake: the sequestered pool, reflecting the quivering trees, with the yellow leaf sleeping on its bosom, and the trout roaming fearlessly about its limpid waters; while some rustic temple or sylvan statue, grown green and dank with age, gives an air of classic sanctity to the seclusion.'

Washington Irving, The Sketch Book of Geoffrey Crayon, Gent., *John Murray, London, 1822*

ANOTHER OLD JOKE

Q: What's brown, sticky and found in the countryside?
A: A stick.

GOD'S COUNTRY

'God made the country, and man made the town.'

Eighteenth-century English poet William Cowper

THE BLUEST BLUE

BRITAIN'S LAST WOAD MILL, in Lincolnshire, closed in the 1930s after the RAF and the police stopped dyeing their uniforms with natural indigo, the pigment that is produced from woad. Now only one commercial woad grower remains in England – Norfolk farmer Ian Howard, who has turned his arable land over to production of the spinach-like plant.

Howard has built a cottage industry around woad, with a visitor centre and woad-dyeing workshops. Norfolk woad, which is used to dye everything from sweaters to towels, appeals to the organic brigade. Apparently you can't find a bluer blue than the blue produced with real woad. Meanwhile, woad seed oil, which is rich in Omega 3, 6 and 9, makes a good moisturiser and is used in soaps and lotions.

Woad fields are cut with a combine harvester. A ton of leaves produces four and a half pounds of dye at around £180 per pound. This is a high-end product – the synthetic version, the type used for dyeing jeans in Manila sweatshops, costs a paltry £1.25 per pound.

CLEAR SKY

England's brave band of wine-growers know the rhyme:

'If on St Vincent Day the sky is clear,
More wine than water will crown the year.'

The fourth-century Spanish martyr St Vincent is the patron saint of vintners, whose day is 22nd January. Vincent's wine connection is hazy. It could simply be a matter of the first three letters of his name. Legend has it that Vincent once stopped by the edge of a vineyard to talk with the labourers. While he chatted, his donkey nibbled (i.e. pruned) the young vine shoots. Next harvest, these vines produced more fruit than all the others.

• There are around 400 English vineyards, producing two million bottles per year. England's biggest vineyard is the 250-acre Denbies at Dorking, Surrey. Unfortunately, EU rules demand that, despite its sometimes inferior quality, English wine cannot be sold cheaper than stuff from the Continent, which means that it tends to be expensive.

102ND USE FOR A DEAD CAT

VICTORIAN GAMEKEEPER JOHN WILKINS, of Stansted, Essex, describes how to trap magpies with a dead cat:

'Take a dead cat, and put it into a magpie's nest when the bird is absent, then make an arbour, close by, to hide yourself in, which you will have plenty of time to do before the bird comes back to her nest to sit. When she returns she spies her enemy the cat, coiled up in her nest fast asleep, as she supposes, and she immediately begins to call out and abuse the cat. She makes such a noise that she soon brings up other flying vermin from the adjoining woods. Don't shoot the mother magpie at first; let her have plenty of time to abuse the cat, and swear at it for being in her nest, thus attracting all her neighbours. These latter, on seeing what's up, perch themselves over the nest and join in a chorus screaming out to awaken the cat and make her quit. Now's your time, when you see a good chance to kill four or five birds together, let fly into the middle of the lot. Down they come at the foot of the tree, and now don't show yourself, but slip another charge into the gun, for the rest will not leave if they don't see you. Very soon they will come and have another try to wake up the cat, and so you get another shot, and kill two or three more.'

The Autobiography Of An English Gamekeeper, Macmillan, 1892

NO BAGGY TROUSERS

'In August and September society people are not supposed to be in town, and therefore if you happen to be in town you can wear country clothes, a thin suit and a straw hat ... because you are passing through on your way to the country.'

'Don't wear brown shoes with a black coat. Brown shoes are intended to be worn in the country and black coats in town; the two do not go well together.'

'If you wear a tweed suit there is no necessity for you to have baggy trousers.'

Nuggets of advice from Jan Barnes, author of Etiquette For The Well-Dressed Man, *Copper Beech Publishing, 1998*

HAND-KNITTED OAT CAKES

Top 10 UK farmers' markets, according to *The Ecologist* magazine:

Winchester, Hampshire: sells everything from ostrich meat and trout fish-cakes, to organic soap made of goat's milk.

Ripley, Surrey: run by volunteers with proceeds going to local causes. Known for special events such as dog shows.

Edinburgh: big on venison, oat cakes and hairy knitwear.

Harrogate, Yorkshire: good selection of regional cheeses and specialities such as Yorkshire rapeseed oil. Vast selection of pies to make you as porky as Eric Pickles.

Stoke Newington, London: only twenty stalls and completely organic as you would expect in this *Guardian*-reading enclave. You know you're in London when a farmer's market sells 'organic ganache stuffed figs soaked in amaretto'.

Gainsborough, Lincolnshire: monthly, held in a shopping centre. Yet more ostrich – does anyone actually eat the stuff?

Stroud, Gloucestershire: good for local cheeses such as Double Gloucester and Stinking Bishop.

Haverfordwest, Pembrokeshire: interesting mixture of produce including low-sugar jams. Excellent dressed crab.

St George's, Belfast: known for its varieties of local sea salt.

Taunton, Somerset: small, and run by a cooperative of local farmers and producers. Big on Indian food made using local produce.

This information first appeared on www.theecologist.org, setting the environmental agenda since 1970

HOLE RULE

The fourth-century writer, Palladius, famous for his immense treatise *Opus Agriculturae*, had the following rule for farmers: 'Dig a hole in the ground. Then try to put the earth back into the hole. If after the hole is filled there is earth left over this means that the soil is rich. If the hole is not full, then the soil is poor. If the earth fits neatly back into the hole then the soil is of middling quality.'

LONGEST

P RIZE FOR THE LONGEST BOOK TITLE pertaining to agriculture and rural management goes to Elizabethan agriculturalist Sir Hugh Plat for his 1594 epic *The Jewell House of Arte And Nature, Containing Divers Rare And Profitable Inventions, Together With Sundry New Experiments In The Art Of Husbandry, Distillation, And Moulding, Faithfully And Familiarly Set Downe, According To The Author's Owne Experience.* This snappy volume includes a vast tract on improving soil with manure. Plat also offers recipes for preserving food in hot weather and how to brew beer without hops. He suggests a cheap way to erect a small bridge over a stream and advises how to keep garments free from moths. And, though goodness knows what it has to do with farming, Plat includes a section on how to guess your opponent's hand at cards.

HOW TO LOOK LIKE A PEAT BOG

'In the country the more you look like a peat bog, the better. A lived-in look, in sludgy browns, greens and cream is the thing. Country suits are tweed, but often a tweed jacket (with only three buttons on the cuff) is worn with cord or cavalry twill trousers. Shirts are often Viyella and can be worn without a tie, and the collar of the shirt stays inside the jacket and is never smoothed out over the lapels. Jeans, shirt and pure wool pullover are fairly standard casual wear. A Barbour (pronounced barber) tops the lot. Shoes are often brown brogues or chukka boots. And if proof were needed of the group nature of dress, the saga of the humble Wellington is it.'

Moyra Bremner, Enquire Within Modern Etiquette and Successful Behaviour, *Hutchinson Reference, 1989*

TIRED

'Don't ride ten miles at a scorching pace, then drink cold water and lie around on the grass, unless you are tired of life.'

Maud C. Cooke, Social Etiquette, *Matthews-Northrup, 1896*

PAINTING COAL

THE BEST KEPT VILLAGE COMPETITION of 1993, with 3,000 entries throughout England and Wales, ended in acrimony after one of the judges described the exercise as 'tainted with suburban values'.

Former headmaster Stephen Friar, a Liberal Democrat councillor in West Dorset and a reluctant appointee to the panel of Dorset judges, accused townies of ruining villages: 'One morning in my village I was awakened by a peculiar noise and there's this huge Volvo in the road and a couple of ladies vacuuming the inside of the village telephone kiosk. Then my school was severely criticised because of the nettles we'd left growing to attract butterflies. One of my council colleagues actually said she'd known people who put bowls of flowers in phone kiosks. ... We do seem to have a preponderance of retired people in the country these days, the great and good from Surbiton and pensioned Army generals, and one senses they've brought with them a tradition of painting coal. They put white-painted stones on verges so tractors don't drive on them.'

Mr Friar described a couple who moved into a local farmhouse from London: 'Next thing I had a distraught phone call saying: "Mr Friar, some deer have escaped from the zoo and they're wandering all over our fields. Do something."'

David Conder, assistant director of competition organisers, the Council for the Protection of Rural England, admitted that 'over-zealous tidiness' had no place in English villages. 'In fact we've issued a leaflet discouraging the gang-mowing of wild flower verges.'

ABOMINABLE BAD MANNERS

ADVICE FROM THE LATE BARBARA CARTLAND
on how to entertain guests in your country house:

- With the shortage of servants and money entertaining has grown not only much less, but much more slipshod. Hosts ask people to 'come and find us as we are', which usually means that they aren't going to take much trouble.
- Few people make their guests really comfortable, mostly because they live uncomfortably themselves.
- With staff: when a guest arrives at an important house his luggage should be carried upstairs and unpacked. If he arrives at 6 o'clock his dinner jacket is put ready on the chair for him to change into. A bath is drawn in the bathroom and a towel put over the chair. Without staff: your husband should offer to carry your guest's case upstairs. Make sure the guest knows where his bath towel is and see that there is a new cake of soap, fresh towels and a *clean* bath mat.
- Be sure your female guest has plenty of coat-hangers in her bedroom and empty drawers. (Clean paper should have been put in these before she arrives.)
- With staff: after dinner the hostess asks the guest what time he would like the butler to call with his breakfast and whether he prefers tea or coffee. Without staff: you will find it far easier for the guest to have his breakfast in bed. It is an awful bother when you are clearing the sitting-room to have someone sitting about. Considerate guests will keep out of the way until latish in the morning.
- Always have a spare hot-water bottle in the house or you will find guests borrowing yours while you lie shivering in bed.
- [Ms Cartland said she suffered so badly from hard beds in other people's houses that she took to travelling with a feather overlay.] It may be doubtful manners to arrive with one, but hosts who sleep on powder puffs themselves give their guests mattresses which haven't had anything done to them for half a century. It is abominable bad manners to make your guests suffer a sleepless night because you are too mean to give them a decent bed.
- Goodbyes. Guests should be seen off on the doorstep by the host or a member of his family. The host waits and waves at the door until the guests have driven off in their cars.

From Barbara Cartland's Etiquette Handbook: A Guide for Good Behaviour from the Boudoir to the Boardroom, *by Barbara Cartland, published by Arrow, reprinted by permission of The Random House Group Ltd*

BATTY

Landowners planning to do work on barns and cottages that might contain bats are committing a criminal offence if they:

1. Deliberately capture, injure or kill a bat.
2. Intentionally or recklessly disturb a bat in its roost or deliberately disturb a group of bats.
3. Damage or destroy a bat roosting place (even if bats are not occupying the roost at the time).
4. Possess or advertise/sell/exchange a bat (dead or alive) or any part of a bat. (Who on earth is going to do this, unless they are a supplier to Shakespearean witches?)
5. Intentionally or recklessly obstruct access to a bat roost.

Not surprisingly, the ludicrously stringent protection of British bats is thanks mostly to European Union law in the guise of the EU's Council Directive on the Conservation of Natural Habitats, better known as the Habitats Directive.

The maximum fine for any of the above is £5,000 per incident or *per bat*. Warning: some roosts contain several hundred bats. You may also receive up to six months in prison, and forfeiture of items used to commit the offence, which in the case of a building company can include vehicles and machinery.

If someone does try to prosecute you for battering a bat, you can plead two defences:

1. You had captured the bat because it looked ill and you wanted to restore it to health and subsequently release it. Ahem.
2. Mercy killing. There was no reasonable hope of recovery (provided that you did not cause the injury in the first place).

HOME HINT

Smoking chimney?
To check whether a bird's nest is causing a blockage, hold a
small mirror in the grate and use it to check if there is
anything up there.

OH, GREENFLY

Greenfly,
It's difficult to see
Why God,
Who made the rose,
Made thee.

Twentieth-century English humorist A.P. Herbert

NOT FOR PETROL HEADS

If you want freedom from petrol fumes, head for Scotland where traffic flows are the lowest in Britain. The lowest of all are in the Western Isles followed by the Highlands, Argyll and Bute, Orkney Islands, Shetland Islands, Scottish Borders and Dumfries and Galloway.

SHEEP NIP

Letter sent to *The Daily Telegraph* in 2010 following the news that a London fox had attacked two children as they slept:

'Sir – Not wishing to trivialise the distressing attack by a fox on two infants, but I was bitten on the knee three weeks ago by a sheep while I was having my lunch at a Peak District beauty spot. A mugshot is available of the perpetrator if a line-up can be formed.

Eva A. Krystek,
Hale, Cheshire'

From I Could Go On, Unpublished Letters To The Daily Telegraph,
edited by Iain Hollingshead, published by
Aurum Press Ltd, 2010

ANGLO-SAXON

The year 2011 came to a close with the news that farmer Keith Coulthard, from the picturesque Cumbrian market town of Wigton, had been fined £200 for erecting a sign on his property warning intruders: 'Do Not Enter. Fuck Off.' According to District Judge Gerald Chalk, the words were deemed likely to case 'harassment, alarm or distress'. It is interesting to learn that rural crime is evidently so low in Cumbria that the county's police have the time, and inclination, to arrest people for expressing sentiments that so many of us in the country feel …

CIVILISATION

'Consider the wheelbarrow. It may lack the grace of an airplane, the speed of an automobile, the initial capacity of a freight car, but its humble wheel marked out the path of what civilisation we still have.'

American nature writer Hal Borland, 1900–1978

TOWNIE MEETS COUNTRY

On being shown a haystack when evacuated to Badminton in 1939, Queen Mary exclaimed, 'So that's what hay looks like.'

NOT QUITE WIDE AWAKE

'FARM-SERVANTS are commonly accused of stupidity and obstinacy. They may not be quite so "wide awake" as mechanics, who, by means of greater intercourse with towns, and latterly through clubs and societies, have more opportunities of acquiring general information. Farm labourers require sharp looking after … Watchfulness is necessary in every department in which they are employed, for they are frequently in a league together to defraud. The ploughman probably has his sweetheart in the house, who will not hesitate to secrete dainties wherewith to pamper her lover; the carter steals corn for his horses, and the thresher for himself; and whether in the kitchen, the stable, or the barn, the utmost vigilance is requisite to guard against the plunder to which an unsuspicious master would certainly be exposed.'

From British Husbandry, *by John French Burke, published 1840: Burke was a well-known Victorian farming author, who wrote the first book aimed at women farmers, titled* Farming For Ladies: A Guide To The Poultry-Yard, The Dairy And Piggery

GREY BRITAIN

Newcastle University researchers say that by 2028, the number of people over age 50 will increase by 47 per cent in rural areas, compared with 30 per cent in towns. The number of rural residents over age 85 is predicted to triple. Rural ageing is caused by young people fleeing to the cities to find work while older people retreat to the countryside for their retirement. The average age of a rural resident is 42, compared with 36 in urban areas.

TROUT'S HEAD REMEDY

Outrageous country cures for a child with whooping cough:

Lancashire: make the child ride on the back of a bear.

Northumberland: put a trout's head into the mouth of the child and let the trout 'breathe' into the child. Another Northumberland remedy was to make porridge over a stream running from north to south and then feed it to the child.

Yorkshire: a tiny bag containing a hairy caterpillar was tied around the child's neck. As the insect died so the cough vanished.

West Country: a man riding a piebald horse was said to gain powers of being able to suggest a remedy. Some time in the nineteenth century, a man was riding a piebald up a street in Cornwall. The people shouted at him, 'What is good for whooping cough?' Losing his patience, the man replied, 'Tie a rope round the child's neck …'

Sunderland: cut off the child's hair and hang it on a tree. The cough was supposed to be 'carried off' by birds who took the hair for their nests.

Devon: the child's hair was cut off and fed to a dog between two slices of bread and butter, thus supposedly passing the cough to the unfortunate dog.

Middlesbrough: the sick child was passed nine times under the belly of a donkey or piebald horse.

Derry, Northern Ireland: typically wacky cure, this one. The patient was given half a bottle of milk, the other half of which had been drunk by a ferret, preferably a pure white one.

PROPER

> O let us love our occupations,
> Bless the squire and his relations,
> Live upon our daily rations,
> And always know our proper stations.

Charles Dickens, 'The Chimes', 1844

PAST SELL-BY DATE

The Spectator magazine agony aunt, Mary Killen, offers essential advice for the squire's wife faced with a tricky situation involving the village ladies:

Question: 'This year I opened our garden to the public in aid of our local church roof. Various ladies were asked to bake cakes to be sold on the day and they did so. Unfortunately, I have since heard that some of the cakes we sold as "Fresh Home-baked Cakes" were, in fact, shop-bought and past their sell-by-dates with the wrappers taken off. How can I prevent this from happening again next year?'

Answer: 'Would it be possible for you to write to all the ladies involved asking them if they might be persuaded to provide cakes? This would afford you the opportunity to include in your letter the following piece of Euroese: "I am obliged by law to mention that due to the new EC regulations all cakes to be sold as fresh and home-baked must legally fulfil these requirements, or their supplier will stand liable to prosecution and a term of imprisonment."'

Reprinted by permission of HarperCollins Publishers Ltd © 1993, Mary Killen,
The Spectator Book of Solutions

TO BE NEARER GOD'S HEART

The kiss of the sun for pardon,
The song of the birds for mirth,
One is nearer God's heart in a garden
Than anywhere else on earth.

Dorothy Gurney (1858–1932): daughter of a London rector, Gurney is best known for writing the hymn 'O Perfect Love' for her sister's wedding; she was not known to be a particularly keen gardener

BIG LEEKS

A survey by a gardening magazine revealed that most people preferred gardening to sex. One in four British women told *New Eden* magazine that they would rather garden than make love, and a third of East Anglians preferred doing the borders than their partners.

Half the UK population put gardening ahead of shopping, playing sport, working out and going to the pub. One in five preferred to mow the lawn than do the washing-up. The report further revealed that 10 per cent of women in London and the South sunbathed topless in their gardens, two-and-a-half times as many as in Scotland, which probably had everything to do with the weather. However, this did not explain why three times as many people in Yorkshire had sex in the garden compared with those in Lancashire. And, incidentally, Yorkshire folk were the ones complaining most about Peeping Toms.

Noisy neighbours were the top garden annoyance, but nobody complained about neighbours sunbathing in the nude. Oddly, two-and-a-half times as many men as women claim to have had sex in their gardens. So, as the magazine pointed out, 'Either the same few women enjoy rolling among the red-hot pokers with a string of different men, or women are less likely to admit to it.'

Amazonian sex symbol and BBC presenter Charlie Dimmock commented that the results came as no surprise: 'Most of my girlfriends prefer to talk about gardening than sex. There's something really satisfying about planning a garden – and it takes longer.'

HANGING ABOUT

'A gentleman visitor who neither shoots, fishes, boats, reads, writes letters, nor does anything but hang about, letting himself be "amused", is an intolerable nuisance. He had better go to the billiard room and practise caroms by himself, or retire to the stables and smoke.'

Mrs John Sherwood, Manners And Social Usages, *1897*

Mrs Sherwood was an American who lectured her readers on how they should behave when in England. She explained that English country house hosts were masters of the 'letting-alone system' of entertaining. Guests were carefully told when they should arrive, and when they should go. 'A man who owns a splendid place near London invites a guest … to come by the three o'clock train on Monday, and to leave by the four o'clock train on Thursday. That means that he shall arrive before dinner on Monday, and leave after luncheon on Thursday. If a guest cannot accede to these hours, he must write and say so. Once arrived, he rarely meets his host or hostess until dinner-time. He is conducted to his room, a cup of tea with some light refreshment is provided, and the well-bred servant in attendance says at what hour before dinner he will be received in the drawing-room. It is possible that some member of the family may be disengaged and may propose a drive before dinner, but this is not often done; the guest is left to himself or herself until dinner.'

PAMPERED BEASTS

'Dogs ... are to be found in a great many houses. In the country, ability to pick up birds (something to do with having soft mouths), chase rabbits, sprawl about in front of enormous log fires and leave hairs on the Savonnerie are usually considered sufficient qualifications to justify the enormous annual expense on Spiller's Shapes, new cushions and paint for the bottom half of every door in the house. (The doors lose their paint because on whichever side of them your dog finds himself he will immediately want to be on the other.) It is rather bad to have only one dog in the country as this makes people think that you keep it purely as a pet – a crime to which one should never admit. It is better indeed to keep six scented Pekingese than one matted Clumber Spaniel since it is always just possible that you hunt martens in Chinese clothes. Guests are obliged to pat and be generally polite to their host's bald, stanching, fourteen-year-old, ill-bred Pomeranians but they must be discreet about slipping biscuits into their noisome maws, as the pampered beasts will either vomit or develop the idea that you are made of biscuit and will attack you, slathering, whenever you make any vaguely affectionate gesture in their direction ... And when bitten to the bone by an ill-tempered whippet, remember to smile wanly as your blood splashes on to the parquet and make some humble apology to its owner, for it is a basic tenet of dog-lore that they can do NO WRONG.'

John Villiers, The Snob Spotter's Guide, *published by*
Weidenfeld and Nicolson, 1958

HOMESICK

OH, to be in England now that April's there
And whoever wakes in England sees, some morning, unaware,
That the lowest boughs and the brushwood sheaf
Round the elm-tree bole are in tiny leaf,
While the chaffinch sings on the orchard bough
In England—now!

Robert Browning (1812–1889), from the poem 'Home Thoughts From Abroad',
written following a bout of homesickness while Browning was living in Italy

NEVER FALL OFF

A random collection of racing terminology:

Age – a Thoroughbred's age is reckoned from 1st January of the year in which it was foaled, irrespective of its actual birthday.

Airing – a horse is 'out for an airing' when it is not expected to win. (Under the Rules of Racing, every horse must be ridden to 'obtain the best possible placing' – i.e. be trying to win, so this is not a phrase commonly uttered by connections.)

Bars – the bars of a horse's mouth are the untoothed gums between the front and back teeth.

Black – a 'black' fence is one that is stiff and solid right up to the very top. With an increasing standardisation in the construction of steeplechase fences, this is more of a hunting term nowadays. (People who think the Grand National fences are formidable should see some of the things jumped by the hunting fraternity.)

Blower – the telephone, particularly when used for betting purposes.

Bone – a horse's bone is his measurement round the cannon bone just below the knee. A big measurement – say nine inches – is 'good bone' and a sign of strength.

Bore – a horse 'bores' during a race when it pushes another off its straight course.

Choppie – chopped hay, or chaff, which is given to a horse to prevent him bolting his hard feed.

Come – a jockey is said to 'come' when he accelerates in a race in an effort to catch the leading horse.

Country – that part of a steeplechase course that is not the main straight is called 'the country'.

Crock – an unsound horse.

Cup – most races have a prize in addition to money, most commonly given in the form of a cup (or plate, sculpture, etc.).

Cut it up – a horse is said to 'cut it up' when it refuses a fence or becomes generally bolshie.

Dog – a horse which will not give its best in a race.

Fall, Fall Off – dangerous ground for the layman. To fall implies that the horse fell and so, of course, the rider did too, possibly despite heroic attempts to keep the partnership upright. Some years ago, point-to-point programmes included alongside a horse's form the initials RFO, or 'rider fell off', meaning that the horse performed splendidly but the jockey was crap. To say a man fell off is to dishonour his name. The catch-all term used nowadays is always 'unseated rider' (UR), which can mean anything from 'rider fell off because crap' to 'rider made heroic attempts to survive a wholesaler blunder by the horse, but gravity won in the end'. Of course, jockeys never like to see 'UR' beside a horse they rode, but there are many shades of meaning.

Field – betting language: all the horses in a race. For example, 'five to one the field' means that all the horses in the race have odds of five to one, or bigger.

Fielder – a punter.

Frog – the india rubber-like portion of the bottom of a horse's foot.

Hands – (a) unit to measure height of horses (a hand is four inches); (b) a jockey possesses 'hands' when he combines sympathy for his horse with delicate touch of wrist and fingers.

Herring-gutted – derogatory term used to describe a horse whose body is flat-sided, running up sharply from the girth and lacking depth of flank.

Hobdayed – an operation on the larynx to improve the breathing of a horse who suffers from partial paralysis in this area, named for its inventor, Professor Sir Frederick Hobday. Fewer horses nowadays are actually hobdayed – there are various techniques (such as the tie-back operation) which have a similar effect – see also 'Make a noise'.

Lad – an employee in a training stable, no matter his age, is a 'lad'.

Make a noise – a horse is said to 'make a noise' if he actually does so when breathing under exertion, because of problems in his lungs or higher up in his respiratory tract. (Early diagnosis of problems in the larynx, and successful treatment thereof, is becoming increasingly common.)

Peck – a horse 'pecks' when it stumbles after jumping a fence.

Penciller – an old term for a bookmaker (they use computers nowadays).

Pony – £25.

Rogue – a horse that won't race or is bad-tempered.

Rubber – a horse grooming duster.

Sheet – a light horse rug.

Springer – a horse whose betting odds shorten very quickly before a race.

Suspensory – a very delicate ligament running down the back of a horse's foreleg.

Wing – the barricades placed either side of a fence to prevent horses from running out.

WOODLAND GIANT

THE MAN WHO GAVE US THE WOODLAND GIANT, the Douglas fir, was a diminutive Scotsman called David Douglas.

Douglas, son of a Perthshire stonemason, was one of the great early nineteenth-century plant collectors. Having trained as a gardener in Scotland, he was hired to search for new species by Royal Horticultural Society secretary Joseph Sabine. While travelling in Canada, in the mountainous region around Vancouver, Douglas discovered the massive fir trees that were to bear his name.

Douglas was a retiring fellow who hated the celebrity that his expeditions earned him. A fellow traveller described him 'a sturdy little Scot, handsome rather, with a head and face of a fine Grecian mould'.

Tragically, an expedition to Hawaii cut short an impressive career. On 12th July 1834 Douglas was taking a mountain trail in the northern part of the island when he disappeared. His gored and trampled body was found at the bottom of a cattle trap occupied by an enraged bull. He was 35. The mysterious circumstances surrounding his death have given rise to speculation as to whether it was an accident, murder, or suicide. Douglas is buried in a cemetery in Honolulu.

> • The tallest tree in Britain is a Douglas fir which towers over Lake Vyrnwy in Wales. It is over 210 feet high, taller than a twenty-storey building.

BLOWING UP WASPS

THE VICTORIAN COUNTRY BOY was a hardy chap, who enjoyed nothing more than messing around with wasp nests. The dubious pleasures of 'wasp-nesting' are explained in the 1859 book *Games and Sports for Young Boys:*

'Every boy ought to know that not a finer bait can be fixed on a fishing hook than the grub of a wasp taken fresh from a wasp nest. But these grubs cannot be obtained without running the risk of being stung, and it is no joke to have a dozen wasps' stings driven into you all at once. We have had our eyes bunged up, and never seen a glimmer of daylight for a dozen hours or more, through wasps stinging us when storming their nests, and yet have been the first to propose storming another nest the week after, for, like all English boys, we had too much pluck to care for a little pain, after the first sharp twinges had passed away. We had been told that wasps could not sting through silk, so, covering our heads with a silk handkerchief, went boldly up to the mouth of the nest. As to the silk protecting us, why their stings went as easily through it as our cavalry went through the Russian troops of horse in the Crimea.'

One way for a small boy to destroy a wasp nest was to blow it up with gunpowder: 'When the powder caught it went hissing deep down into the interior of the nest and caught beautifully. But the wasps seemed to care no more for the burning powder than a duck does for a shower of rain; they came out with a rush that was so strong that they forced up the turf, which was placed over the hole. Though the boys were armed with branches, with which they knocked down scores of wasps, hundreds more joined the attack, and we had to run for it, many of us carrying the enemy with us on our necks.'

TIP FOR THE COUNTRY HOUSE WEEKEND

'If visiting a friend for a short stay never take a trunk so big that it suggests the possibility of an indefinite lingering.'

Margaret Sangster,
Good Manners For All Occasions, *1921*

STARS

Britain's top star-gazing spots, as recommended by the National Trust:

Bignor Car Park, Slindon Estate, West Sussex: remarkably free from light pollution; a high point on the top of the South Downs.

Black Down, Sussex: highest point of the South Downs; huge night sky.

Buckstones Car Park, Marsden Moor, Yorkshire: high on the spine of the Pennines; easily accessible by road, yet remote enough to avoid light pollution.

Divis Mountain, Belfast, Northern Ireland: on the northern edge of Belfast reaching 1,562 feet with little to obstruct the view.

Dunkery Beacon, Holnicote Estate, Exmoor: highest point on Exmoor, with sweeping skies; best spot is about half a mile from the car park along a rough track.

Echo Mount, Knole, Kent: the top of Echo Mount, situated near to the house in Knole's deer park, provides a good viewpoint; easy access from London.

Godolphin Hill, Cornwall: conical hill offers 360-degree views with no artificial lights nearby.

Lake District, Cumbria: looking down to Derwent Water, framed by fells and mountains, Friar's Crag is a peaceful place to observe the night sky.

Headley Heath, near Boxhill, Surrey: a popular spot with astronomers who consider Headley Heath to be one of the best places in Surrey for star-gazing.

Lake District campsites, Cumbria: all three campsites lie in unique locations – Low Wray on the western shore of Windermere; Langdale at the head of the Langdale valley; Wasdale at the head of the Wasdale valley in the quiet Western Lake District. Very dark at night and perfect for viewing the Perseid meteor shower.

Leith Hill Tower, Surrey: highest point in south east England; steep steps up from car park.

Mam Tor, Peak District, Derbyshire: Bronze Age hill fort offers clear, unobstructed views of the night sky.

Penbryn Beach, Cardigan, Wales: the golden sands of Penbryn are perfect for star-gazing and are reached through the woods of a fern-clad valley. Look out for seals at dusk.

Rinsey Cliff, Cornwall: A southerly aspect with no artificial lights.

South Milton Sands, South Devon: fantastic, peaceful spot away from the intrusion of lights. Spectacular sunsets.

Staple Plain, Quantocks, Somerset: perfect for the disabled since the car park at Staple Plain offers a great place to view the stars.

Stonehenge Landscape, Wiltshire: possibly the best place in England for star-gazing since the monuments are directly connected to the skies above, with stones aligned to moonrises and moonsets. Expect a spiritual experience. Stonehenge car park closes in the evening, but it is possible to park nearby.

Teign Valley, Devon: wide-open skies above Piddledown Common.

Trelissick Park, Trelissick Garden, Cornwall: far enough away from Truro to avoid light pollution; panoramic views.

Wicken Fen, Cambridgeshire: skies don't come much bigger than here.

Winchelsea, East Sussex: snug hilltop setting above flatlands of Sussex and Kent. Surprisingly dark at night, considering its southern position.

OUT OF TOUCH

The quirky ways of country folk: as if to say that the countryside can go eff itself, Prime Minister Gordon Brown in 2009 appoints a fellow Scot, former Glaswegian fireman Jim Fitzpatrick, as Minister for Food, Farming and Environment. Fitzpatrick represents an East London constituency and is a vegetarian who has barely glimpsed mud. His immediate superior is Environment Secretary Hilary (Wedgwood) Benn, who doesn't eat meat either and, again, is utterly metropolitan just like his father, the old leftie Holland Park-dwelling toff Anthony. Brown has a final insult up his sleeve – he appoints Dan Norris, an avowed townie, as the new rural minister. The closest Norris gets to the countryside is spending his weekends with anti-hunt campaigners spying on packs that might be breaking the law.

WEIGHT IN GOLD

Oak logs will warm you well,
If they're old and dry.
Larch logs of pinewoods smell
But the sparks will fly.
Beech logs for Christmas time;
Yew logs heat well;
'Scotch' logs it is a crime
For anyone to sell.
Birch logs will burn too fast;
Chestnut scarce at all;
Hawthorn logs are good to last
If cut in the fall.
Holly logs will burn like wax,
You should burn them green;
Elm logs like smouldering flax,
No flame to be seen.
Pear logs and apple logs,
They will scent your room;
Cherry logs across the dogs
Smell like flowers in bloom,
But ash logs all smooth and grey
Burn them green or old,
Buy up all that come your way
They're worth their weight in gold.

Anon

There are several variations of this old rhyme. All woods burn better when
seasoned and some burn better when split.

VEG

'When I am in the country I wish to vegetate like the country.'

Nineteenth-century essayist William Hazlitt

FARMER GEORGE

SATIRISTS DUBBED KING GEORGE III (1760–1820) 'Farmer George' for his love of farming.

Described as a simple man of 'plain, homely, thrifty manners and tastes', George much preferred the countryside to the town. 'I certainly see as little of London as I possibly can', he wrote in 1785. 'I am never a volunteer there.'

George played a significant role in the British agricultural revolution that was reaching its peak by the time of his reign. He spent his days on the Crown Estates at Richmond and Windsor. At Richmond he kept an experimental flock of British sheep crossed with Spanish Merino. His favourite spot was Kew Gardens, where he experimented with crop rotation. Rather than handing over his acres to the tenantry, as had been the habit of the upper classes in the past, George kept his in hand. Thanks to his influence, farming became a respectable occupation, worthy of the gentry.

George was a typical farmer in that he seldom travelled anywhere. He was quite the bumpkin. He never visited Scotland, Wales or Ireland. The furthest he went from his beloved Kew was a short holiday to Cheltenham in 1788. The king's remarkable lack of adventure was put down to his preference for a life of strict routine.

• King 'Farmer' George learned of his nickname after meeting a peasant one morning who was driving a flock of sheep towards Windsor. The king stopped to look at them, and asked who they were for.

'For Farmer George', came the reply.
'And who is Farmer George? I thought I knew all the farmers in this neighbourhood.'
'He lives at that great house yonder', said the peasant, pointing at Windsor Castle. 'Zum volks calls un the King, but we calls un Farmer George.'
The king was delighted.

• George III was one of the first farmers to give his labourers grain and milk at a cheap fixed rate.

• Towards the end of his life, George suffered from severe mental instability caused by the hereditary disorder porphyria. Ever the country lover, he once disembarked from his coach in Windsor Great Park in order to shake hands with an oak tree which he thought was Frederick the Great.

COUNTRY DESPAIR

I don't want the river, the smell of the gorse,
The trees, or the fools on the stupid golf course.
I'm tired of the forest, the sound of the sea,
I hate all the things that spell Country to me!
I'm longing with almost a wicked despair
For London and all the dear things that are there.
I want to meet someone who'll talk of a play,
Or the latest new book, or the man of the day.
I want to hear music, a verse read aloud,
I want to enjoy an intelligent crowd.
I want to see pictures, and go out to dine,
AND NEVER AGAIN CAST MY PEARLS BEFORE SWINE!

'The Country Wife', by Elizabeth Paget: this poem appeared in The Perfect
Hostess, *by Rose Henniker Heaton, published by Methuen and Co. Ltd, 1931*

SOME THOUGHTS ON GAME

'It is not possible to lay down any hard-and fast-rules about the right moment
to eat game. It depends entirely on the weather and the state of the birds (if
badly shot, or if old, or young). If a bird is old, it keeps longer, and is better
for keeping so long as it is dry and not mauled in any way. Of course, late in
the season the birds keep much longer. Woodcock, snipe and plover, should
be eaten fresh. The great thing is slow cooking, and plenty of basting:

> Grouse – keep a few days if weather permits.
> Pheasant – hang four to five days if weather permits.
> Partridge – keep a few days if weather permits.
> Wild duck – keep a few days if possible.
> Wild pigeon – eat fresh.'

Rose Henniker Heaton, The Perfect Hostess, *published
by Methuen and Co. Ltd, 1931*

SMALL IS BEST

BRITAIN'S TEN BEST SMALL COUNTRY TOWNS, according to rural pundit and *Country Life* Editor at Large Clive Aslet:

1. Framlingham, Suffolk (pop. 3,000). Renowned for its excellent shops and market in a pristine 'heritage' setting. The Co-op supermarket is so cleverly tucked away that only locals know of its existence.
2. Presteigne, Powys (pop. 2,000). Small streets, old-fashioned shop windows and cheap property.
3. Beverley, East Yorkshire (pop. 33,000). Stupendous architecture with an abundance of Georgian terraces. The Minster is a church of cathedral proportions.
4. Louth, Lincolnshire (pop. 15,000). A classic Georgian town with orderly streets in the beautiful Lincolnshire Wolds. Louth has been described as 'a perfect focus for rural life'.
5. Whitby, North Yorkshire (pop. 14,000). A pretty town of fishermen's houses and pantiled roofs, clustered around a harbour. The abbey ruins formed the setting for *Bram Stoker's Dracula*.
6. Ludlow, Shropshire (pop. 10,000). Once the administrative capital of Wales, Ludlow has, in recent decades, reinvented itself as a flag-bearer for local food. It remains small enough to see the glorious countryside of the Welsh Marches beyond the chimneys of the handsome Georgian houses of a country town which contains everything needful for a civilised life.
7. Berwick-upon-Tweed, Northumberland (pop. 12,000). England's defence against Scotland. Solid stone houses built to keep out the Northumberland weather. You can see the nearby beaches from the spectacular Tudor ramparts.
8. Market Harborough, Leicestershire (pop. 21,000). Bustling but charming commercial town set in fine, farming countryside: a good hunting base.
9. Ramsgate, Kent (pop. 38,000). A seaside charmer. Quality Street architecture: stucco-fronted, bow-windowed, with ironwork verandas and balconies.
10. Elgin, Morayshire (pop. 21,000). An outstandingly civilised town, in its rather high-minded Scottish way. Bargain house prices.

STEREOTYPES

William Cowper's 1785 portrayal of a gypsy camp in his long poem 'The Task', with verses that these days would be considered extremely non-PC:

I see a column of slow-rising smoke
O'ertop the lofty wood that skirts the wild.
A vagabond and useless tribe there eat
Their miserable meal. A kettle, slung
Between two poles upon a stick transverse,
Receives the morsel—flesh obscene of dog,
Or vermin, or at best of cock purloin'd
From his accustom'd perch. Hard-faring race!
They pick their fuel out of every hedge,
Which, kindled with dry leaves, just saves unquench'd
The spark of life. The sportive wind blows wide
Their fluttering rags, and shows a tawny skin,
The vellum of the pedigree they claim.
Great skill have they in palmistry, and more
To conjure clean away the gold they touch,
Conveying worthless dross into its place;
Loud when they beg, dumb only when they steal.
Strange! that a creature rational, and cast
In human mould, should brutalise by choice
His nature; and, though capable of arts
By which the world might profit, and himself
Self-banish'd from society, prefer
Such squalid sloth to honourable toil!
Yet even these, though, feigning sickness oft,
They swathe the forehead, drag the limping limb,
And vex their flesh with artificial sores,
Can change their whine into a mirthful note
When safe occasion offers; and with dance,
And music of the bladder and the bag,
Beguile their woes, and make the woods resound.
Such health and gaiety of heart enjoy
The houseless rovers of the sylvan world:
And, breathing wholesome air, and wandering much,
Need other physic none to heal the effects
Of loathsome diet, penury, and cold.

A GREAT PROPORTION OF BAD PLAYERS

THE JULY 1866 EDITION of *Blackwood's Edinburgh Magazine* offers this insight into the game of country house croquet:

'On the croquet ground the proportion of bad players is generally so great that everyone seems perfectly satisfied with his or her performance; and the most helpless bunglers (usually being ladies) become objects of affectionate interest to their more skilful partners … In many points the croquet ground affords as apt illustrations of the great game of life as the more familiar type of the chess-board. The players make stepping-stones of their friends and their enemies alike to further their own ambitious projects, and will sometimes sacrifice the humble interests of a friend in the hope of disappointing the schemes of an enemy. The more hoops a player can contrive to work himself through, the more sure he is to find eager friends to take him on to the next, and carry him to the goal in triumph. The only analogy in society is in the case of the scamp of the family, whom every relative is anxious to get into some safe place, that he may be no longer a scandal to the name. And it must be sometimes felt that if, as at croquet, he could be taken up to the stick, and killed dead at once, it would be the best thing for all parties.'

• It has been said of croquet that only tobacco smoke spread faster through the British Empire.

• Croquet became a one-off Olympic sport at the Paris Summer Olympics in 1900. Croquet holds an important place in Olympic history since seven men and three women – it was the first Olympic event that women could enter – took part. Every medal was won by France, which is not surprising, as the only non-French competitor was a Belgian who failed to complete the first round. In what appeared to be a Gallic fix, the event was made nearly impossible for foreigners to enter as the competition began on 24th June and continued only on Sundays until 15th August. It was so badly organised that one of the competitors didn't realise he was competing in the Olympics but thought he was taking part in some local French league.

• An amusing way to liven up country house croquet is to place mousetraps strategically around the hoops. If your ball sets off a mousetrap you are sent back to the start.

ADVICE IN SPADES

The National Council for Metal Detecting Code of Conduct:

1. Do not trespass. Obtain permission before venturing on to any land.

2. Respect the Country Code, leave gates and property as you find them and do not damage crops, frighten animals or disturb nesting birds.

3. Wherever the site, do not leave a mess or an unsafe surface for those who may follow. It is perfectly simple to extract a coin or other small object buried a few inches below the ground without digging a great hole. Use a suitable digging implement to cut a neat flap (do not remove the plug of earth entirely from the ground), extract the object, reinstate the grass, sand or soil carefully, and even you will have difficulty in locating the find spot again.

4. If you discover any live ammunition or any lethal object such as an unexploded bomb or mine, do not disturb it. Mark the site carefully and report the find to the local police and landowner.

5. Help keep Britain tidy. Safely dispose of refuse you come across.

6. Report all unusual historical finds to the landowner, and acquaint yourself with current NCMD policy relating to the Voluntary Reporting of Portable Antiquities.

7. Remember it is illegal for anyone to use a metal detector on a designated area (e.g. scheduled archaeological site, SSSI, or Ministry of Defence property) without permission from the appropriate authority.

8. Acquaint yourself with the Treasure Act 1996 and its associated Code of Practice, making sure you understand your responsibilities.

9. Remember that when you are out with your metal detector you are an ambassador for the hobby. Do nothing that might give it a bad name.

10. Never miss an opportunity to explain your hobby to anyone who asks about it.

The following finds are classed as treasure under the 1996 Treasure Act and must be reported to the local coroner within fourteen days:

- All coins from the same hoard. A hoard is defined as two or more coins, as long as they are at least 300 years old when found. If they contain less than 10 per cent gold or silver there must be at least ten in the hoard for it to qualify.
- Two or more prehistoric base metal objects in association with one another.
- Any individual (non-coin) find that is at least 300 years old and contains at least 10 per cent gold or silver.
- Associated finds: any object of any material found in the same place as (or which had previously been together with) another object which is deemed treasure.
- Objects substantially made from gold or silver but less than 300 years old, that have been deliberately hidden with the intention of recovery and whose owners or heirs are unknown.

The following are NOT classed as treasure and can be kept with impunity:

- Objects whose owners can be traced.
- Human and animal remains.
- Objects from the foreshore which are wreckage.
- Single coins on their own.
- Groups of coins lost one by one over a period of time.

WITCH'S BUSH

A 'besom' is a birch twig 'witch's broomstick'. Besoms were traditionally made by 'broomsquires'. As well as being general yard brooms, besoms were used by butchers and fishmongers to whisk away flies, and by carpet makers to brush away fluff. The 'bush' in The Old Bull And Bush was a besom. Innkeepers hung them outside their doors to indicate they brewed their own ale – besoms were used to stir fermenting beer since the twigs became impregnated with yeast, thus encouraging the fermentation process.

- Useless broom info: the core of small birch twigs that make up a broom is known as 'snuffings'. A 'swale' is a short-handled birch brush.

TRACTOR FACT

The only person to have been run over by a tractor at a rock festival is Raymond R. Mizzak, 17, who was crushed to death in his sleeping bag in a muddy parking lot at Woodstock (1969) shortly before Sly and The Family Stone went on stage.

IN PRAISE OF HAWTHORN

'The hawthorn … makes a hedge so well furnished with thorns as to be quite impenetrable to cattle. The branches burn as well green as dry, and are often used in heating ovens; the tips of the young shoots are used to adulterate tea; the bark furnishes a yellow dye, and with copperas, is used to dye black. It is scarcely necessary to describe the appearance of this plant, since it forms the common material of hedges in the neighbourhood of towns as well as in the depths of the country, and is one of the first plants on which we perceive the tender green foliage of spring. Its white and fragrant blossoms too! Who is unacquainted with them, named as they are from the lovely month of May? The village May-pole, that relic of old times, is not yet quite forgotten, nor are the May-day garlands of village children yet neglected; but vainly have we looked for some years past for the true "May", or hawthorn blossoms, on May-day. The hawthorn must not, however, be passed over as a mere hedge-plant, for when allowed to grow to its natural size it forms a handsome bush, and in old age a picturesque and gnarled tree, very pleasing to the eye.'

Sarah Tomlinson, Sketches of Rural Affairs, *published 1857*

EASY

'There are three easy ways of losing money: racing is the quickest, women the most pleasant, and farming the most certain.'

Lord Amherst (1717–1797), Governor General of British North America

A FULL CHURCH

FOLLOWING THE DREADFUL PLAGUES AND FAMINES of the 1300s, villagers solved the problem of declining rural congregations by demolishing an aisle or two of the parish church. Could we not do the same today? It would save a fortune in maintenance and heating. And would it not be gratifying at Sunday service to see a full church, even if it was on the small side?

NEAR CAT-ASTROPHE

PRIZE FOR BRITAIN'S MOST UNOBSERVANT FARM CAT goes to Smokey, a County Durham moggy, who in 2009 gave birth in a combine harvester. The machine had already been started in preparation for the harvest when a farm worker discovered three kittens inches from the blades. 'The teeth in the crushing mechanism are incredibly sharp', farmer Shane Dew reported. 'How anything so soft and delicate survived is amazing.'

MISERABLE FAILURES

A splendid rant by Victorian angling author Cornwall Simeon on the vexed subject of stuffed fish:

'Judging from the miserable failures which constantly offend the eye, it would appear that the art of stuffing fish is one in which it is very difficult to attain a result at all approaching perfection. So-called preserved specimens are almost invariably stuck straight up in the middle of their cases: fins and tail stretched to the utmost possible limits; eyes, the largest that can be forced into the sockets, and guiltless of any attempt at speculation; body often stuffed out like a 'roly-poly' pudding; and the colour generally toned down to a rich deep mahogany. And all this without the slightest accessories of weed or stones to relieve the barren dreariness of the case.'

From Stray Notes on Fishing and Natural History,
by Cornwall Simeon, published 1860

THE BEAUTY OF TURF

'There can be no item more recurrent to human eyes than grass, yet, in proportion to its constant reappearance, there can be no form of life which receives less attention from the passer-by. Just as to the great Dr Johnson one green field was like another green field, so to most people grass is just grass, something that cattle eat or something that man can turn into lawns. They do not realise the infinite variety of growth in every yard of turf or the infinite beauty of the individual flowers: the crowded spike-like inflorescences of the foxtail, the trembling florets of the quake-grass, the wild proud panicle of the oats. There is no greater competition for existence anywhere than in a meadow. Even human footsteps will encourage those grasses which prefer a firm tilth, to the detriment of those who like a looser soil. Hence the clearly marked line of a footpath, where the grasses which thrive happen to be of a dark colour.'

Twentieth-century Irish artist and author Robert Gibbings

HOW TO AMUSE SMALL BOYS ON A DULL AFTERNOON

'To intoxicate and take fish. Make a paste in the following manner: take *cocculus indicus*, cummin seeds, fenugreek seeds, and coriander seeds, equal parts, reduce them to powder, and make them into a paste, with rice flour and water; reduce this paste into small balls of the size of peas, and throw it into such ponds or rivers where there are fish, which, after eating thereof, will rise to the surface of the water almost motionless, and will allow themselves to be taken out by the hand.'

The New Family Receipt Book, *1810*

RUDE DOG

Following the Labradoodle and Cockapoo, a new fashionable crossbreed of country 'designer' dog has emerged in the Shires. A combination of Staffordshire Bull Terrier and Shi Tzu, it is known as the Bullshit.

PRETTIEST

THE POET WILLIAM WORDSWORTH declared that the 'prettiest field in England' was at the head of Ullswater by Patterdale, Cumbria. A natural arena, the backdrop was part of the mighty Helvellyn, the Lake District's third-highest fell. The field is now known as the King George V playing field and is home to Patterdale Cricket Club. In August Wordsworth's paradise is host to the famous sheep dog trials known as Patterdale Dog Day.

BRITAIN'S GREATEST HISTORICAL MONUMENT

The Campaign to Protect Rural England was established in 1926 in order to protect the 'beauty, life and uniqueness' of the British countryside. The spread of the big cities was out of control and the middle-classes felt it was time to stop the urban sprawl.

Their saviour was Sir Patrick Abercrombie (1879–1957), a town planner who was to bring us the 'New Town' concept of combining housing with green open spaces. Abercrombie loved historic country towns set in traditional English landscapes. His article headlined 'The Preservation Of Rural England' in a dull, but worthy journal called *The Town Planning Review* was to act as a catalyst for the foundation of the Council for the Preservation of Rural England.

Far from calling for a ban on all building in the countryside, Abercrombie pleaded for moderate levels of rural development: 'The recluse who lives in the country and

the town dweller who uses it as a recreational contrast to his ordinary existence ... both these would probably like to see (the countryside) sterilized or stabilized in its present state and all development prevented.' But sensible planning was needed in order to preserve the beauty of the countryside. 'It is not safe to leave these changes to adjust themselves, hoping that somehow a general harmony will result from individualistic satisfactions. It should be possible for a just balance to be struck between conservation and development.'

Sir Patrick declared that England's 'greatest historical monument' was its countryside and all the market towns, villages, hedgerows, trees, lanes, copses, streams and farmsteads contained therein: 'To destroy these and leave a considerable number of archaeological specimens neatly docketed and securely fenced off from a wilderness of slag-heaps or rubbish tips might satisfy the unadulterated antiquarian, but the plain man would lose his greatest possession – the country setting.'

Abercrombie is best known for his work on the 1944 Greater London Plan, described as the greatest open space strategy ever formulated for a capital city. The idea was to create a web of open space leading from the city centre, through green corridors to a 'green belt' on the periphery.

This green belt would effectively halt London at its 1939 limits. And beyond it would lie no fewer than eight of Abercrombie's so-called New Towns, although in the end only two were eventually built, Harlow and Crawley.

• Abercrombie was co-founder of the CPRE's Welsh equivalent with radical architect Clough Williams-Ellis, designer of fake Italian fishing village Port Meirion on the north Wales coast.

• The CPRE claim that each year about twenty-one square miles of English countryside is built over with buildings or roads.

• As of 2011 the President of the CPRE was American anglophile author Bill Bryson, who has settled with his family in Norfolk. He has described England as 'this wondrous place – crazy as fuck, but adorable to the tiniest degree', and has written of Blackpool: 'On Friday and Saturday nights, it has more public toilets than anywhere else: elsewhere they call them doorways.'

• Members of the CPRE are sometimes unkindly dubbed as Aga Louts because of their lack of understanding of the true countryside. Their reputation has not been helped by the fact that from 1997 to 2002 the CPRE president was actress Prunella Scales, star of TV commercials for Tesco, a company generally loathed by farmers for its aggressive pricing policies. Aga Louts were summed up in a damning 2001 article in *New Statesman* magazine:

'Aga Louts have always had a problem with yeomen whose cows moo at night or shit in the lanes. ... The truth is that many Aga Louts dislike farmers because they envy their busy lives, the sense of unending usefulness dictated by the seasons. With his suburban tennis court and stockyard swimming pool conversion, the Aga Lout wants the landscape to enhance, rather than detract from, the accessories and fantasies of his own pointless life. He likes to play farm, fencing open paddocks to keep his pets in and rambling peasants out. ... The Aga Lout also prides himself on a finely tuned social conscience, the need to conserve the "traditional" values of the peasant culture his presence has undermined. He cares about low-cost housing (so long as its proximity does not detract from the value of his property), the village shop and post office, the rural bus service, none of which he uses, preferring to drive his gas-guzzling 4x4 to the urban supermarket fifteen miles away. Coffee mornings for the blind, the sclerotic, the Conservative Party and other disadvantaged or endangered species (Aga Louts are almost always New Labour) enable him to catch up on the latest in house prices and the incompetence of Old Villagers who are employed as charladies to scrub their floors or as gardeners to mow their croquet lawns. Farmers and other Old Villagers are, it goes without saying, not invited to these social gatherings. Aga Louts will protest that they have introduced acceptable standards to the rude simplicities of English rural life. How else would Dungpong-cum-Blasterheath have learnt to love the canapé and cocktail culture of Islington Person, to worship the ill-tempered chefs creating exotic metropolitan dishes in one-time cider houses?'

Peter Dunn, New Statesman, *2001*

SQUIRREL CRIMINALS

Owners of suburban gardens tempted to trap grey squirrels and then dump them in the countryside should be aware that this is a criminal offence. Under the Wildlife and Countryside Act, 1981, it is against the law to catch a grey squirrel and then re-release it back into the wild. A Gloucestershire vicar who in 2009 trapped a squirrel in his loft was astonished to learn that he could not release it in the local woods. The Reverend Douglas Drane had to pay a pest control expert £70 to put the animal down (although, at the risk of offending more sensitive readers, one has to wonder why he didn't simply thwack it on the head with a shovel.)

Other animals which the law says cannot be released into the wild include: sika and cervus deer; fat dormouse; European tree frog; common wall lizard; Mongolian gerbil; prairie dog; Italian crested

newt; Himalayan porcupine; black rat; red-necked wallaby; every sort of crayfish you can think of.

• Britain's five million squirrels cause more than £20 million worth of damage to homes every year, including gnawed roof beams and chewed wiring. Most insurance companies do not cover squirrel infestation. As of 2011 squirrels in Britain were out of control, with an estimated 50,000 houses occupied by Nutkin and his chums. One couple who fell victim to this menace were Glen and Laura Borner, whose three-bedroom Hertfordshire home burned down after the little bastards chewed through electrical wiring in the loft. Other ways that squirrels can ruin your life include contaminating water tanks with their droppings and munching through water pipes. The best way to stop them is to block any holes in the building and to ensure that trees are far enough from the house to stop them leaping onto your property. You can also try putting down chilli powder at possible entrances – squirrels hate the smell of anything spicy. Squirrels avoid Indian restaurants.

• The Forestry Commission estimate that squirrels cause more than £10 million of damage to woodland trees each year. Prince Charles, patron of the Tree Register, hates squirrels because they cause terrible damage to hardwood trees by stripping the bark.

• Grey squirrels are native to north-east

America. They were first released into the wild in Britain in 1876 by misguided animal lover Thomas Brocklehurst, who thought they looked cute in woodland. Cheshire landowner Brocklehurst had no idea of the problems he would cause. (Brocklehursts are not good with wildlife. Henry Courtney Brocklehurst, cavalry officer and big game hunter, had the distinction in 1935 of becoming the first person to shoot a giant panda.)

• The first grey squirrels in Scotland were released at Loch Long in 1892. Within twenty-five years the animals had spread over an area of 300 square miles.

• The Department for Environment, Food And Rural Affairs (Defra) is developing an oral contraceptive for grey squirrels. The squirrel pill should be available by 2016. Critics say this is a daft waste of money. What Defra do not seem to have got the hang of is that squirrels store food in caches for later use. What happens when other birds and animals find the food store? Of course, any countryman with half a brain knows that the only way to deal with the squirrel plague is by shooting them in a nationwide cull. All farmers receiving agricultural subsidies could be required to control squirrels on their land. But don't expect that suggestion to come from successive British governments which seem to cower in terror at the fluffy-bunny lobby.

• The endangered red squirrel is heavily protected and it is an offence to kill, injure or take a red squirrel, or to damage or obstruct access to a red squirrel drey.

• It was fashionable in late Georgian England to keep a pet squirrel. Children suffered frequently from bitten fingers.

COW CRAZY

'DOES ANYONE ELSE FIND IT AMAZING that during the mad cow epidemic our government could track a single cow, born in, say, Appleby, Yorkshire, almost three years ago, right to the stall where she slept in the county of Cumbria? And, they even tracked her calves to their stalls. However, the Government are unable to locate 125,000 illegal immigrants wandering around our country. Perhaps they should give each of them a cow.'

Anon, from a 'viral' email doing the rounds of the internet, 2011

LEY LINE LORE

LEY LINES are so-called alignments of ancient sites and holy places across rural Britain. New Agers convince themselves that our ancestors built their sites in straight lines dependent on mysterious energy forces within the earth.

The phenomenon known as ley lines surfaced in 1922 with the publication of a book called *Early British Trackways*, by Alfred Watkins, a businessman and self-taught amateur archaeologist. Based on the fact that on the map of an area near Leominster, Herefordshire, he could link a number of ancient landmarks by a series of straight lines, Watkins became convinced he had discovered an ancient trade route.

Nearly a century later, New Agers claim that the world is littered with ley lines linking 'spiritual' sites such as Stonehenge, Mount Everest, Ayers Rock and the Great Pyramid at Giza. However, there is absolutely no hard, scientific evidence to support this theory other than what one observer has described as 'subjective certainty based on uncontrolled observations by untutored devotees'.

• The word ley is a variant of lea, meaning grassland, clearing, or pasture. On this basis, the less than spiritual Dudley rests on a ley line.

• UFO nuts believe flying saucers use ley lines for navigational purposes.

• Ley line enthusiasts believe that any pub called the Red Lion is situated on a ley line.

• The Seattle city authorities have given $5,000 to a group of dowsers called the Geo Group to draw a ley line map of the city. The Geo Group say, 'The vision of the Seattle Ley-Line Project is to heal the Earth energies within the Seattle city limits by identifying ley-line power centers in Seattle, neutralizing negative energies and then amplifying the positive potential of the ley-line power centers. We believe the result will be a decrease in disease and anxiety, an increased sense of wholeness and well-being and the achievement of Seattle's potential as a center of power for good on Spaceship Earth.'

DENTALLY CHALLENGED

'Country people have worse teeth than Londoners.'

Novelist, magazine person and social pundit Nicholas Coleridge

IDEAL

The saying goes that in the perfect country home the cooking would be French, the plumbing German, the decor Italian, and the gardeners English.

TOUGH TROUT

Enjoy thy stream, thou little fish,
And should some angler for his dish
Through gluttony's vile sin
Attempt – the wretch – to pull thee out
God give thee strength, thou little trout,
To pull the rascal in.

Satirist John Wolcot (1738–1819)
writing under his nom-de-plume
of Peter Pindar

TEASING CLOTH

Britain's most obscure farm crop is teasel, a spiky flower that is used for raising the nap on fine cloth. There are still a couple of teasel farms in Somerset selling their hand-picked produce to Edmund Taylor Ltd, Britain's last remaining teasel dealer in Huddersfield, the traditional centre of the teasel industry. Most teasel these days is grown in Spain and France, although the British variety is said to be the best.

Fuller's teasel (*D. fullonum*), a type of Dipascus, is used to give a velvety surface to fine cloth used in billiard tables, Guardsmen's tunics and Rolls Royce roof lining. The plant remains in demand in the Scottish cloth industry. But whereas most textile processes have been mechanised, no machine has managed to do a better job. Artificial metal teasels produce a far inferior finish.

The teasel process involves up to 4,000 flower heads mounted on rods on a rotating drum known as a gig. The gig spins slowly over the taut surface of the cloth. The stiff needle-like bracts just below the flowers cause the fibres to stand up so that they form a pile, or 'nap'. This is shaved and pressed to create a silky smooth fabric such as billiard table cloth. Mounting teasels in a gig frame is a highly skilled job. The burrs are used twice, once on either side, before being replaced.

A field of teasels in flower resemble thistles. Cutting begins in the first week of August and is done using a crescent-shaped knife. An experienced cutter can harvest 10,000 stems per day. An average crop yields about 200,000 heads per acre. Bundles are placed on poles, where they are dried. This is done carefully in an open shed to prevent moulding. They are then packed into bales and sent to the teasel dealer, who trims and grades them before selling them on to the cloth mills. The largest teasels are known as 'kings', the medium-sized flowers are 'queens' and the smallest are 'button' teasels. The quality of the teasel is measured in its elasticity, retention of spines and wearing qualities, characteristics greatly influenced by soil and climatic conditions.

• Teasel is an Anglo-Saxon word related to the word tease, referring to the disentangling of fibres. The name of the flower Dipascus comes from the Greek and means a little cup for holding water. This cup – known as the Venus basin – is found at the base of the teasel leaves. In the Middle Ages girls believed that drops of water collecting there possessed cosmetic properties and could remove warts, wrinkles and freckles.

• The Romans used hedgehog skins to raise the nap on cloth.

• Somerset teasel production was traditionally centred on the three villages of Curry Rivel, Fivehead and Curry Mallet. The teasel crop, which takes two years to grow, was often undersown with coriander and caraway.

• The teasel trade became a hotbed of industrial action in the 1790s with the introduction of the gig mill. Until then, raising the nap on cloth had been done using a hand-held device set with teasel heads. Teasel shearmen were the labour aristocrats of the textile industry. They were the best paid and most militant of all the cloth-making trades. Towards the end of the eighteenth century, mechanised teasel devices threatened to put shearmen out of business. The shearmen staged strikes and the industrial unrest culminated in the 'Wiltshire outrages' of July, 1802, when a group of men burst into an isolated mill at Littleton, near Trowbridge, and set it on fire causing £8,000 worth of damage. Thomas Helliker, a 19-year-old shearman's 'colt', or apprentice, was arrested and charged with arson. He was found guilty and hanged. His burial place was marked with a tombstone erected "To the memory of the Trowbridge Martyr'.

KNOW THE FEELING?

QUOTE BY AUGUST GRIMBLE, great Victorian sporting writer, who maintained there was nothing worse than to return after a day's salmon fishing having caught nothing:

'To come home blank is the abomination of desolation. To work hard at anything the whole day for nothing does not suit our temperament, for after such an event, dinner is not enjoyed, sleep fails us, breakfast next morning is hateful, and peace of mind and content can only again be restored by a tight line and the music of the reel.'

POPULAR AMONG THE INFERIOR ORDERS

'I do not know a finer race of men than the English country gentlemen. Instead of the softness and effeminacy which characterise the men of rank in most countries, they exhibit a union of elegance and strength, a robustness of frame and freshness of complexion, which I am inclined to attribute to their living so much in the open air. ... The man of refinement finds nothing revolting in an intercourse with the lower orders in rural life as he does when he casually mingles with the lower orders of cities. He lays aside his distance and reserve, and is glad to waive the distinctions of rank, and to enter into the honest, heart-felt enjoyments of common life. Indeed, the very amusements of the country bring men more and more together; and the sound of hound and horn blend all feelings into harmony. I believe this is one great reason why the nobility and gentry are more popular among the inferior orders in England than they are in any other country.'

From Godey's Lady Book, *a nineteenth-century American women's magazine published in Philadelphia: Godey's considered itself the 'queen of monthlies'*

BLOW BACK

A story is told in Scotland of an elderly angler who asked that, after his death, his ashes be scattered in his favourite pool. There was a strong wind on the day of the ceremony. When the lid of the urn was lifted the ash blew back into the faces of the mourners. 'Och!', exclaimed the head ghillie, 'He always was an awkward bugger.'

- Not long ago, a well-known Midlands match angler stated in his will that, following cremation, he wanted his ashes balled up like groundbait and thrown into his favourite local water. His mates complied.

MUCKY

As New Labour headed for the political rocks in 2009 there was much excitement amongst the landed gentry at the news that, far from focusing on the 'privileged' backgrounds of his Tory opponents, Labour party supremo Lord Mandelson had at last obtained a pair of Wellington boots. Not any old ten quid, black mucker-outers either, but some splendid leather-lined numbers from Le Chameau, the type seen on all the best shoots. The boots were a birthday present from Mandelson's author friend Robert Harris, and Mandy was able to show them off a couple of weeks later at a shooting party on the Oxfordshire estate of billionaire Lord Rothschild.

- The Wellington boot was the creation of the 1st Duke of Wellington, who instructed his London shoemaker Mr Hoby to modify the standard eighteenth-century hessian boot. The result was some elegant footwear made in soft calfskin and cut close around the leg. It was hard-wearing enough for the battlefield as well as looking rather stylish. The rubber version of the boot was created by Victorian entrepreneur Henry Lee Norris who, in 1856, launched the North British Rubber Company at a factory in Edinburgh. This subsequently became the Hunter Rubber Company, makers of Hunter gumboots.

LIFE WITH SHEEP

The late agricultural pundit James Wentworth Day (1889–1983) told a story of a shepherd he encountered while researching his 1943 travel book *Farming Adventure: A Thousand Miles Through England On A Horse.* The shepherd, something of a loner, was evidently highly intelligent.

> 'You think a lot', Wentworth Day remarked.
> 'If you spend all your life with the sheep under God's heaven you *must* think, sir,' the shepherd replied. 'I've laid rough half my life. If you live like that, you *know* there is a God above.'

• The slot of a shepherd's crook must be the width of the hind leg bone of a sheep. The end must be curved and blunted so it does not harm the animal.

PLOUGHMAN

'Break a field and make a man.'

Old English farm saying

SAVOURY STRIPY

BRITAIN'S LONGEST-RUNNING COUNTRYSIDE FEUD is the battle between livestock farmers and badger conservationists over whether badgers should be culled. The anti-badger brigade insist that the animals spread tuberculosis among cattle, while badger lovers claim this is nonsense. Meanwhile, governments refuse to make up their minds for fear of upsetting anyone. While the debate drags on, here is a recipe offered as a treat for the more feral reader:

Badger ham: a badger ham weighs seven to eight pounds and demands careful cooking. Soak the ham for at least six hours in cold water. Wash it after soaking in lukewarm water. Cover it with a rough paste made with three pounds of flour and two-and-a-half pints of water; make sure to wrap it well. Bake in a moderate oven, pre-heat to 350° F for two-and-a-half to three hours. Remove the paste and cover with breadcrumbs whilst still hot. Serve with broad beans and cider sauce.

If you try this, you will have to do so abroad since animal protection laws make the eating of badgers illegal in the United Kingdom. *And that includes road kill.* The Badger Protection Act states: 'A person is guilty of an offence if … he has in his possession or under his control any dead badger [one wonders whether it is possible to possess an *out-of-control* dead badger] or any part of, or anything derived from, a dead badger.' This includes badger steaks, badger chops, badger burgers, badger pies, goujons de badger, etc. However, they devour badger kebabs in Russia (perfect after a night out on the voddie) and, in Croatia, Brock ends up in goulash. The French create an enticing stew called *blarieur au sang.* The Chinese, who seem happy to eat anything with four legs except the table, are said to favour sweet and sour badger.

• Badgers were traditionally regarded as being at their fattest and culinary best from October to November. Until badgers became protected in 1992, some West Country pubs kept a ham on the bar. Badger is said to taste a bit like young pig.

THE PIG'S NUMBER TWO-ER

Rules for playing conkers:

Make a hole through the centre of your conker. Thread a strong piece of string through the hole and tie a knot at one end, so that it doesn't pull through.

Players take turns at hitting their opponent's conker. If your conker is to be hit first you hold it at the height your opponent chooses. Your opponent tries to hit your conker with his. If the striker misses he is allowed up to two more goes.

If the strings tangle, the first player to call 'strings' gets an extra shot.

If the striker hits his opponent's conker so that it completes a whole circle – 'round the world' – after being hit, the striker gets another go.

If a player drops his conker, or it is knocked out of his hand, the other player can shout 'stamps' and jump on it.

The game goes on in turns until one of the conkers is destroyed.

A winning conker is known as a 'one-er'. Its beaten opponents' scores are then added to its own score. For example, a 'one-er' beating a 'two-er' becomes a 'three-er', and so on.

- The best way to grade conkers is to put them in a bucket. The ones that have damage inside them will float, but the good ones will sink to the bottom.

- Dastardly prep school tricks for hardening your conker:
    - Soak it in vinegar, salt water or paraffin.
    - Bake it in an oven for half an hour. (Best not whilst soaked in paraffin!)
    - Store an old conker in the dark for a year and it will harden up nicely.
    - Fill your conker with glue.
    - Coat your conker with clear nail-varnish.
    - One for conker nutcases only – let a pig eat your conker and then collect it at the other end. The conker will be hardened by the pig's stomach juices.

- The World Conker Championships are held each October on the village green at Ashton in Northamptonshire. To prevent cheating, contestants are not allowed to use their own conkers. If neither conker has broken after five minutes, each player has three sets of three hits and the one who lands the most clean hits is the winner. Contestants come from all over the world, including Mexico.

• Conker (horse chestnut) trees were first introduced to England in the late sixteenth century from Eastern Europe.

• The first recorded game of conkers was on the Isle of Wight in 1848 and was modelled on a fifteenth-century game played with hazelnuts. The word 'conker' stems from either the word 'conqueror' or the French word *cogner*, meaning to hit.

• Folklore says that you should carry a conker in your pocket to help prevent piles and rheumatism. They can also be used in wardrobes to discourage moths.

FOOLISH FISHING

'Fly-fishing may be a very pleasant amusement; but angling or float fishing I can only compare to a stick and a string, with a worm at one end and a fool at the other.'

English essayist Samuel Johnson (1709–1784)

HORRIBLE

After an uncomfortable journey through his newly acquired domain following the Roman invasion of Britain in 55BC, a dispirited Julius Caesar remarked that England was nothing more than 'one horrible wood'.

NO TORTUR'D WORM

The most memorable verses in praise of fly-fishing were written by English poet and dramatist John Gay (1685–1732). Gay penned these lines in his epic 1713 poem 'The Rural Sports':

Around the steel no tortur'd worm shall twine,
No blood of living insect stain my line;
Let me, less cruel, cast the feather'd hook,
With pliant rod athwart the pebbled brook,
Silent along the mazy margin stray,
And with the fur-wrought fly delude the prey…
Mark well the various seasons of the year,
How the succeeding insect race appear,
In their revolving moon one colour reigns,
Which in the next the fickle trout disdains;
Oft have I seen a skilful angler try
The various colours of the treach'rous fly;
When he with fruitless pain hath skimmed the brook,
And the coy fish rejects the skipping hook.
He shakes the boughs that on the margin grow,
Which o'er the stream a weaving forest throw;
When if an insect fall (his certain guide)
He gently takes him from the whirling tide;
Examines well his form with curious eyes,
His gaudy vest, his wings, his horns, his size.
Then round his hook the chosen fur he winds,
And on the back a speckled feather binds;
So just the colours shine through every part,
That nature seems to live again in art.

• John Gay loosely modelled 'The Rural Sports', a poem of 443 lines, on Virgil's *Georgics*: as a dramatist he is best remembered for *The Beggar's Opera* (1728)